LIFE AFTER LIFE

Tony Parker was born in Manchester in 1923. His many books include *The Courage of his Convictions*, *Lighthouse*, *The People of Providence*, *Soldier Soldier*, *Red Hill*, *A Place Called Bird* and *May the Lord in His Mercy be kind to Belfast*. He and his wife live in Suffolk.

Tony Parker has been described (by Richard Heller in the *Mail on Sunday*) as 'among the world's most brilliant inter-viewers'. Anthony Storr in the *Independent* has written: 'No one has ever used the tape-recorder with greater virtuosity than Tony Parker. He never passes judgement and never talks down; so that the habitually inarticulate become almost eloquent, and the insulted and injured feel that, perhaps for the first time, they can talk freely to someone who really understands them.' According to John Keegan in *The Times*, 'Tony Parker has the sort of power over a tape-recorder that Cartier-Bresson had over a camera – a mesmerist's gift.'

'The nearest most of us will get to understanding the mind of a murderer is through the pages of Tony Parker's extraordinary new book . . . Parker's book raises questions about the treat-ment of lifers' CLARE COLVIN, *The Sunday Express*

'The vast majority of normal people will, I believe, weep several times in the course of reading these astonishing confessions . . . Parker can detect gold in a slagheap. With this new collection, he has found hope amidst the horror of self-hatred . . . through all the squalor of human sin, there is humour, wit, hope and goodness in these pages'
BRIAN MASTERS, *The Literary Review*

'You have to make your own mind up about these murderers - which means coming to grips with yourself in uncomfortable ways' VICTORIA GLENDINNING, *The Times*

Further reviews overleaf

LIFE AFTER LIFE

TONY PARKER

Life After Life

Interviews with Twelve Murderers

HarperCollins*Publishers*

HarperCollins*Publishers*
77–85 Fulham Palace Road,
Hammersmith, London W6 8JB

This paperback edition 1994
3 5 7 9 8 6 4 2

First published in Great Britain by
Martin Secker & Warburg Ltd 1990

ISBN 0 00 638352 1

Printed in Great Britain by
HarperCollinsManufacturing Glasgow

The lines on page vii are from 'Poem for Spain',
from *Collected Shorter Poems* by W.H. Auden;
those on page 146 are from *Four Quartets* by T.S. Eliot.
All extracts are quoted by kind permission of Faber & Faber Ltd.

In memory of my father
Tom Handford Parker

and for my children
John, Kristen, Tom, John and Tim

with love

History to the defeated
May say Alas but cannot help or pardon

W. H. Auden

Contents

Preface   xi

1   No problem   1
    DANNY MORGAN

2   Pretty well the whole story   19
    EDGAR JOHNSON

3   Tears don't count though do they?   39
    CAROL BOWEN

4   A perfectly ordinary normal person   59
    PAUL ARROWSMITH

5   The life and times of an inadequate psychopath   79
    ARTHUR DODDS

6   A man with no history   97
    ANDY REID

7   You do still wonder sometimes   115
    VALERIE SCOTT

8   Big Bully Billy   133
    WILLIAM DAVENPORT

9   Something terrible has happened   151
    PHILIP DERBYSHIRE

10   My story   169
    BETTY DREW

11   The theory of deterrence   195
    ALAN ROBINSON

12   Marathon Man   215
    FRANK JONES

Acknowledgements   233

Preface

A person convicted of murder will be sentenced to imprisonment for life. It is the only sentence the law allows, and the trial judge has no option but to pass it. It remains in force until the day the person given it dies, and it can never be cancelled or revoked. 'For life' means for life.

A lifer may however at some stage be allowed out of prison on licence, to continue serving the sentence in the community under the supervision of a probation officer, on strict conditions. Such conditional release only occurs after lengthy consideration by the Parole Board, and usually not before several years have passed. Final permission for it can only be granted by the Home Secretary. It is not by any means automatic: currently thirty-eight life sentence prisoners have so far been in custody for more than twenty years (in one case for almost forty years).

Conditional release on licence in no way resembles 'freedom'. You have to report to your supervising probation officer where, when and how often he or she says. At the beginning it will probably be on a weekly basis: but it could be daily. After several months this requirement may be relaxed to once a fortnight: possibly after a further period to once a month and perhaps, after some years, to once every three months. At any time the probation officer may alter the frequency and increase it again, depending on your situation and his or her assessment of your behaviour and progress.

Additionally, you can't move without permission from where you're living, and you have to accept visits from the probation officer as often as you're required to. You cannot change your job or leave it without permission, nor can you go abroad on holiday. Stricter control still is exercised over your personal freedoms: if your probation officer says so, you must inform your employer, actual or potential, that you're a life sentence prisoner on licence and describe the circumstances of the offence for which you were convicted if they're considered relevant. (If you wanted to take a job in a restaurant kitchen, for example, and had previously committed murder by stabbing someone with a knife.) Most intrusive of all, some feel, is the obligation that if you become involved in any kind of growing relationship with another person of the opposite (or the same) sex, you not only have to tell your probation officer, but must also tell the other person concerned of your conviction and the circumstances of it. Reassurance on your part that you've done so will not be accepted: the probation officer will insist on meeting the other person involved, and confirming with them that they're in full possession of the facts.

You are liable to be recalled to prison instantly and without further trial if your probation officer considers you're not abiding closely enough to any or all of the licence conditions. You will then serve more of your sentence back in custody, until such time (which can be several years) as the Parole Board decides to release you on licence again. This means in fact that as a life sentence licensee, you can at any time be taken back to prison not only for something you've done, but for something it's considered you may possibly do. (If for instance your original offence had been killing somebody in a drunken brawl, and you then at some time after release began drinking again and became involved in a fight; or if you'd killed someone in a fit of jealousy, and then again became entangled in a strongly emotional involvement.)

Detailed reports on your circumstances, situation, behaviour and response to supervision are sent once every three months by your probation officer to the Home Office. The purpose of this is twofold: to monitor your progress or lack of it, and to oversee how your probation officer is handling you. Any shortcomings on either side are promptly pointed out.

And of course if you're ever convicted by a court for an offence which in type seems to have any similarity at all, however remote, with that which previously led to your committing murder, your recall to prison will almost certainly automatically follow. Justification for recall, whether it's for an offence or what's considered to be the possibility of one, has to be confirmed to you by the Home Office: but you have no opportunity of waiting to see what will be decided. Confirmation or otherwise does not occur until after you're back in custody.

Usually after about four or five years of completely trouble-free existence in the community, if your supervising probation officer considers your readjustment and reintegration warrant it, permission may be sought from the Home Office to relax the conditions of your licence. It may or may not be granted. But if it is, the life sentence still remains, and you are and always will be liable to have the conditions reimposed, or to be recalled to prison. At every stage of life licence supervision, the primary consideration is not the welfare of the person on licence, but the Home Office's estimation of the degree of risk to the public presented by the offender.

According to current (1993) Home Office figures, about 2,500 people (out of a prison population of 47,000) are at present in custody serving life sentences for murder. It is estimated that about a further thousand are out in the community on licence. During the last ten years an average of fifty-seven murderers a year have been released on licence; and on average seventeen a year are recalled. The caution with which the whole subject is handled is indicated by the fact that over the past fifteen years, of all the people who have been released on licence from sentences of life imprisonment for murder (about 900), only seven have been convicted of murder again.

T.P.

ONE

No problem

DANNY MORGAN

He rapped smartly on the half-open door and came briskly and confidently into the sparsely furnished spare room on the top floor of the old Victorian house where the local Probation Service's offices were. Small, young, fair haired, brown eyed, dapper in a green bomber jacket over a clean white T-shirt and jeans. His hand was held out ready for shaking, and he kept on smiling and winking and nodding his head.

– Hello, how do, sorry I'm late it's the buses, they're never too clever in the afternoons. Nice to meet you, my pleasure.

His voice was staccato almost, but level toned: it stayed fixed while his eyes darted round the room, taking in the two old office chairs, the table, the empty cupboard, the unused filing cabinet and last year's NACRO poster calendar on the wall.

Which one do you prefer, no it doesn't to me either, I don't mind either way. Shall I sit in this one then? Well not what you'd call all that posh surroundings eh, still it's warm that's something. Mind if I take my jacket off? I've never been here up in the attic before, usually it's Terry's office on the first floor. He said this'd be best, we'd be out of the way up here and no one'd disturb us. Yes well if it's all right with you it's all right with me as far as I'm concerned. I don't know, that chair you're on, it looks a lot more wobbly than this one to me, should we do a swap? No all right if you're happy I'm happy.

About coming to see you, well as far as I'm concerned there's no problem, no problem at all. I mean I can make it Monday Tuesday next week, whenever you say. Just to suit you. That's until I get myself fixed up with a job naturally, then I'd have to see what my hours were and work it round those. Well I should say that'd be in two or three weeks. I mean that's according to what Terry says it'll take him to find me something. Matter of fact I've got an interview for one later this afternoon after I've seen you, just round the corner here: baker's van driver I think it is, something like that. No there's no problem, he said they said I could drop in any time up to six o'clock or even a bit after. Before we start, did Terry say there was any chance we might get a cup of tea? Well I'll pop down to his office and ask him a bit later on shall I? So then right, I'm ready to start in straight away if you are.

No I've already thought it over all I need to. As far as I'm concerned there's no problem about talking to you, none at all. Terry's explained to me you're talking to about twelve or fifteen people is it who've all done lifes, and then you'll put it all in a book with names changed and all the rest of it. He says you're very reliable, so that's good enough for me, I'm perfectly happy about it. He's a good bloke Terry, if he says something's OK then as far as I'm concerned it's OK, know how I mean? 'Advise, assist and befriend you', that's what they say your probation officer's for isn't it? Tell you the honest truth, I thought he was a bit of a prick the first time I met him, but he's not, he's a nice bloke. I have to see him every week to start with, but then in a bit if he's satisfied with me it could start getting less.

He understands my home circumstances and so on, that's why he said we could use here for our talks. Oh, didn't he tell you? Sorry, my mistake, I thought he'd filled you in with my whole background and everything. Well what it is you see, is I'm thinking about how my mam and dad would take it if they knew I was talking to somebody about it all. It's the one subject we never mention at home you see, we all think it's better that way, I mean not to talk about it. They know I come and see Terry I mean, because they know I have to, being let out on licence and all the rest of it. But I'm not telling them about talking to you, they think I'm just coming to talk to Terry.

I mean don't get me wrong, I've not got anything to hide from them. They've been very good to me which is why I don't want to do anything to upset them you see. People get funny ideas: if they knew I was talking to you they might think I was trying to hide something so it's better they don't know. Just for a start I mean, I'll see how it goes. I'm not saying I won't tell them eventually, or perhaps quite soon even, but not straight off until they've got used to the idea.

I mean the idea of having me back home with them again. It's only been four weeks since I came out of prison so things need time to settle down don't they, it's only natural isn't it? That was why they moved to live in a new area and everything, ready for me coming home, complete fresh start sort of idea. I can appreciate it from their point of view, they don't want to have to start straight away telling everyone their son's just come home from doing six years for killing his grandfather do they?

– Yes I've done what you said last week and thought some more about it, how it might make difficulties for me or upset me and things. I still feel the same though, I'd like to go ahead and do it, that's if you feel it'd be of help. Well I mean help to you in what you're doing, and help to other people in helping them to understand people who kill people. Help to me? Oh yes it'd be that too definitely. Terry says it would: I respect his opinion. You see it's not something you can talk to everybody about is it? I mean I like to be friendly with people and all that sort of thing, but it's not something you can sort of go up to someone in a pub is it, and say 'How'd you do, my name's Danny Morgan, I'm a murderer'? No, right, yes, no you definitely can't.

So then make a start today then shall we, right, where'd you want me to begin? No I don't mind, however you like, you're the boss, we'll do it whatever way you say. Well if you're asking me personally what I think, then I think I suppose the best way would be to start at the beginning, would it, sort of work on and take things from there? Right then that's how I'll do it.

Well I suppose the first thing's to say my name's Danny Morgan, which you already know, I'm twenty-one years of age, and I came out of prison exactly five weeks tomorrow. At the moment I'm living here in Blackburn with me mam and dad, at their house which they came to live at just before Christmas. I've been in prison seven and a half years which is a long time, specially for someone my age, but I'm settling down nicely outside; or at least according to my probation officer Terry I am, and I think so too. I'd never been in prison before in my life for anything, and I shall never go back to prison again because I'm not what could be called a criminal sort of person.

Yes that's right, perhaps we should make that clear at the start shouldn't we? Right, well I committed my offence when I was aged fourteen, just over in fact, and you can't be given a prison sentence as young as that so what I got is what's called HMP. That is sentenced to be detained at Her Majesty's Pleasure which means an indefinite period: it hasn't got a fixed length to it, it's until they decide they're going to let you out again. It depends on when you're considered no longer to be a danger to the community I suppose. In my case what happened was I was sent first to a treatment centre for young offenders called St Andrews, and then after a few years when I was old enough I was sent on to a borstal, or a youth custody centre's what they call them now. That's more like a proper prison and then I was given my discharge from there. I liked the youth custody centre better than the St Andrews youth treatment place because there seemed to be more point to it: St Andrews was just a sort of psychiatric hospital, all you did was sit around all day and talk.

I've run on a bit now. I said I'd try and keep things more or less in order didn't I? Can you ask me a question or something that'll put me back on the right lines?

As far as that? Well there's not a lot I can remember about my childhood really, I suppose you'd have to say it was just an ordinary sort of a one, nothing much special about it at all. I had two sisters, well stepsisters really because my mam had been married before, and I think I remember I had all the usual things like measles and chicken-pox and all the rest of it. Just an ordinary sort of kid, a bit small for my age which I still am now. I didn't like school very much, this was in Birkenhead, my father was a fitter I think in the shipyards. I used to steal sweets from shops but I mean all kids do that don't they? I wasn't much different from anyone else in that way. Oh there was once I remember though when the police caught me for stealing a rug or something from a car, and I got taken to court and given a talking-to, bound over, that's all. But it wasn't anything big if you know what I mean. Most kids do little things: some get caught and some don't, that's all it amounts to really.

I'd say we were mostly a normal family on the whole. We didn't have a lot of money, we lived in one of those what they call back-to-back terrace houses, council houses they were. The one we had was near the end of the terrace, then my other sister who was married had another one a few doors down, and then next to that my grandad lived. We were a sort of little family group all close together you could say. My grandad? Well he lived on his own, his wife had died quite a few years sooner I think, I don't know much about her. He'd be about sixty-nine or seventy I suppose. I liked him, he was a nice man, he used to take me on the ferry across to New Brighton and things like that. He was a kind man, he had white hair round the back like this, and a jolly face. It was a shame about what happened, I was very sad about it after. I'd say myself what happened was mostly an accident really, in the sense I didn't mean to kill him. I mean I meant to hurt him yes, but not kill him, I felt bad about that.

It was a Friday afternoon after school. I wanted my pocket money or I wanted some more pocket money, I'm not sure now which it was. But my mam wouldn't give it me, so I thought if I went round and told him my grandad would. But he wouldn't and we had a big argument about it. He was sitting at his kitchen table and there was a pair of scissors on the table, and I lost my temper and picked them up and stabbed him with them a couple of times in the neck, just about there.

Then I ran out of his house and ran away.

– Last time, talking about being sad. Yes, well I have thought some more about it yes. The way I think about things now, is that it happened, it's over and done with and there's not much point now in dwelling on it. I think this is the right way to look at it. I'm sorry he's dead because I liked him, but there it is, he's gone and like I said I look on it it was like an accident, something that could have happened to anyone.

I'm sorry I don't think I'm with you: what could have happened to anyone, how'd you mean? Oh, I see, yes which do I mean could have happened to anyone, the killing or the being killed? Well both I suppose. I mean the scissors lying there on the table, they needn't have been, it could have been a spoon or something. Or them sticking into him where they did in his neck, it could just as well have been his shoulder or his chest or somewhere round here where it couldn't have done the same damage. Or I suppose if I hadn't drunk a whole can of beer a bit earlier. That was all it needed with me, I was fourteen and I'd no head for it at all, one pint and I'd be under the table. So if I'd had less to drink, or even if I'd had more to drink and been incapable, I probably wouldn't have done it either way would I? Yes or if he'd given me the pocket money, you could say that's true as well. I wouldn't say I was a quick-tempered person normally no, I mean that's one thing it did teach me at St Andrews, how to keep your temper under control.

Anyhow, I'll go on now right, shall I? Last time we stopped where I ran out of the house, yes. Well I ran out of the house because I was very very frightened. I ran like buggery. I mean I knew I was going to get into trouble, I mean that was obvious wasn't it? I didn't know he was dead of course, but I could see from the way he fell he must have been badly hurt. So I ran and ran. Not far away from the houses where I lived there were some fields, and then like beyond those there were some woods and I ran into those. Later on it started to get dark, but it was summer and it wasn't very cold, and I didn't want to go home so I went to sleep under a hedge in a field. Well it was just over a wall in a churchyard actually, in the cemetery. I wasn't really hiding or anything, I think I was mostly in what they call a state of shock is it? One of the things I've never worked out in my mind is why the police didn't come looking for me, they'd easily have found me. But they didn't and they didn't pick me up until well on into the next morning when I was walking along a lane. This police car stopped and the coppers said 'Come on son' and they put me in the car and took me to the police station and that was that.

They sent for my mother and she came down, and I gave them an admission straight away of what I'd done and they wrote it down and I signed it. The way they wrote it down it made it sound very callous but it wasn't really like that. I remember my mother didn't say much to me, but she looked very shocked about it.

I was taken off to a remand centre and kept in custody to await trial. I got very very impatient because they kept taking me to court and having me remanded again, and I wanted to get on with it and have it over. It went on for months, I was remanded twenty-one times in twenty-one weeks, that's six months nearly. My father and mother came to see me pretty regular, and sometimes my sisters came. Only there was never anything much to talk about. I could never think of anything to say and neither could they, we all got pretty fed up with all that waiting. My parents sent me in some of those models to do, you know plastic models of motor cars and aeroplanes and things, and they passed the time. When you're on remand you don't have to work but after a bit I volunteered to go and help in the stores, just because it was something to do.

In the end though I got up to court eventually, and I pleaded guilty. I mean I was guilty wasn't I, there couldn't really be an argument about it. Everybody at the remand centre'd told me I'd get HMP, there couldn't be any other sentence, and that's what I got. Most people when I asked them guessed I'd probably do round about seven or eight years, and that was what I made up my mind for. Then after the trial it was back to the remand centre for assessment tests while they made up their mind what to do with me. That took them nearly another whole year, then finally I was told I was going to St Andrews Treatment Centre which was specially for young people with my kind of offence.

I thought it was a rotten place to be honest with you about it. All group meetings every day and people interviewing you, everyone all the time asking you stupid questions. 'Why did you say such and such in the group meeting?' was one; and then the other one was if you just sat there with your mouth shut 'Why didn't you say anything in the group meeting?' It was enough to drive you barmy: a lot of the people there were, specially the staff.

'Why did you kill your grandfather?' Well yes they were always asking me that one. Well I didn't know, did I? I thought that was why they'd sent me there, to find out. But I couldn't tell them, and they couldn't tell me, so the question never got answered did it?

– Yes I'll go back on last week for you, course I will. You know, like I said, I'm doing this to try to help you: anything you don't understand and you want me to explain it again, I'm only too happy to try and oblige. No, my pleasure.

So then: that St Andrews Treatment Centre place, why I didn't think it was any good, and the borstal and why I thought it was better. Let's see if I can spell it out a bit clearer then.

St Andrews, to be perfectly honest with you about it, for me I think it was a complete waste of time. The way I looked at it, what had happened had happened, it was over and done with, and all I wanted was to get on and do my time for it, and then come out with it all behind me and forget it and get on with my life. I think there was about twenty-six or twenty-eight kids there altogether boys and girls, with ages about thirteen to seventeen. They'd not all done murders, I think there was only three or four of us who had: but most of them had done pretty serious sorts of stuff, arsons or rapes or stabbings, attempted poisonings and things like that.

Now you see me, I'm the sort of person who if he's in a situation, a job, a prison sentence or whatever it is, he likes to get on with it to the best of his ability and not have hassle or give it either. I like to be friends with people, I like to have a smile on my face, and a laugh and a joke with whoever it is I'm with. Take me in a pub and I'll get on with everyone who's there: doesn't matter if they're my age, a few years younger or a lot older, you know how I mean? 'Hallo Danny how are you, how's life treating you then?' 'Oh I'm fine chum, everything's great, no problems at all, how's it with you?' That's how I like it to be, nice and easy and smooth, just like that. Even though I'm saying it myself, I am an easygoing person and one who it's very easy to get on with. Whoever you ask, they'd all tell you that: my dad, my mam, my sisters, everyone. I'll bring for you next week if you like reports on me from the work training places I went to, you can read them for yourself. They say I like to try and be pleasant and friendly and helpful: I don't go around picking quarrels with people, or things like that. Life's too short, that's what I say: if people take me like I am, I won't give anybody trouble, I'll be polite and cheerful and well behaved from morning till night.

Only well at St Andrews they didn't want that. Everybody had their problems and all they wanted to do was talk about them. And the staff, well that's what they wanted everyone to do too. They were always trying to quarrel with you or upset you: I don't mean in a nasty way, they weren't cruel or anything of that sort. But they were all the time how can I put it, well I suppose the only word's encouraging you and everyone else to lose their tempers and shout and scream and all the rest of it. It was like the more everybody quarrelled with everybody the happier they were, do you understand me? And then afterwards there'd have to be a big inquest about it. It would be sort of something like: 'Now come along everybody, this morning we're going to talk about why Tina called Gregory a shit yesterday. Now you keep quiet Gregory and let's all hear from Tina why she called you a shit, Tina why did you call Gregory a shit? OK now you still keep quiet Gregory, let's hear first from everybody else if they think it was right Tina called Gregory a shit. Is he a shit? Right, anybody got anything else to say? So OK well let's hear now from you Gregory, you've heard other people's opinions, what's yours: do you think you're a shit?'

They could make something like that last a whole morning, even a whole day. I could never see what good it was, and I either used to lose my temper or just switch off. Complete waste of time, horrible atmosphere, big rows all about nothing; that's what it was, it was really shocking. Everybody used to say if you weren't barmy when you came in, you would be before you were let out, that was one thing was absolutely sure.

So after what would it be, nearly three years of that, you can imagine what a relief it was to be sent to a borstal. That was run on proper lines, it was more or less the same as an ordinary prison. I shouldn't keep calling it a borstal by the way, the name now's youth custody centre. Most people who're in them still do go on using the old name though. Anyway, there you knew exactly where you were: the rules and regulations set down, and they were simple and straightforward and no messing. You got up at a certain time, then you went back to your dormitory or your cell, then you went to your work, then dinner, then exercise, more work, then tea, evening association and watching TV, and then at the end of the day you were banged up. Always exactly the same each day except for a bit of leeway at weekends say. If you kept your nose clean and got on with your work and didn't get in fights, no one bothered you: if you stepped out of line and broke the rules, you knew what would happen to you. You took your punishment and when it was over then that was the end of it.

The borstal I was at, it wasn't a cushy number, nothing like that, in fact it had the reputation of being one of the tougher ones. Tough but fair, know what I mean? Quite a lot of physical exercise and marching about, but I quite enjoyed that. I liked the people who ran it, they were straight down the line people: you don't give us no trouble and we won't give any to you. It was really all right I'd say, really all right it was.

– Well the best thing about the borstal I was telling you about, it was getting my date obviously. When you're doing a life or an HMP, that's really all you're thinking about from the day you start. You know how I mean, when are they going to give me my date of release? There's not a day or a night you're not thinking of it, because that's the day when you can say it's stopped being an indefinite sentence and become a definite one. It doesn't matter how far away it is in the future, you've got a target to keep your eyes on, something you're counting down towards every minute that goes by. For me, my date when they gave it me was almost I think about a whole full year ahead; but from then on, once I knew it everything I was doing was aimed on that.

They sent me out on two of those what they call work preparation courses, they were pretty good. One was a sort of a social skills sort of thing where they teach you about everyday experiences and how to handle them, how to behave and so on; the other was more actual work, simple jobs like say for a canteen assistant or packing up parcels, so when you do go out you won't be a person who hasn't had any experience of anything. At St Andrews I'd only been out for a day a couple of times: but you always had to have a member of staff with you, one to one. But these were residential courses, I think one was for three days and the other one a week. You go on your own and get yourself back on your own, so you have experience of travel on buses for instance or trains. Oh and on top of that I did something else of my own too: I'd saved up my money from work while I was inside, and I finally got enough together to pay for having driving lessons, so they let me go out for those as well. I did well, I really studied and practised hard at it, and I passed first time.

My worst moment in the whole of that last year at the borstal? Without any doubt, that was when I got a knock-back and they took my parole date off me. It was my own fault, I did a very stupid thing to bring it about. Towards the end of your time they'll let you out a few hours or half a day even on your own; I went out and I told you I've no head for drink, so what did I do but go in a pub and get drunk, and go back late. That was the end of my privileges: they took my release date off me and said I'd got to learn how to be responsible. I was lucky, they only put it back eight weeks so it wasn't as bad as it might have been. But it upset me a lot. To think I'd got so near and then it looked as though I'd thrown everything away, I can tell you it really upset me. All the good behaviour and everything, I felt terrible. Still all that's in the past now.

Oh yes that reminds me, those reports I was telling you about that I had when I went on the courses, I had a look when I got home last night: I found one I'd still got a copy of, I've brought it along. Read it out loud you mean? Yes certainly. It's got the name of the training place here at the top then my name underneath. 'Danny Morgan has success-fully completed his course with us, and he has been an excellent trainee in every way. He is a very gentle and patient young man, very pleasant and helpful and always ready to be of assistance to others.' We are sure he will do well in the future and wish him good luck and success. Signed E Morrison, Manager.' That wasn't bad was it, to get something like that? I mean it's not exactly what you might call a job reference, but you never know when it might come in handy. You'd have to be a bit careful who you showed it to, that's all.

Well it's from a job training centre you see isn't it? That

means anywhere if you're going asking for a job, as soon as you show them that, you're telling them you've been unemployed a long time. Then naturally they ask you why: in my case I'd have to say I've been in prison, then they ask what for, and that's when it starts getting awkward doesn't it? I know if you've done a life sentence you're supposed to tell a prospective employer that anyway officially; but I mean a lot of it depends on the sort of job it's going to be. If it's say a milk roundsman or something of that sort, I don't suppose it matters that you should tell them straight off about it: you could put in a few weeks' work before you brought it up so they'll see you're a good worker first, know how I mean?

Sometimes for a change we went to a tea bar over the road. It had cramped bench seats and dark red formica-topped tables, and we always went right to the back, from where he could see any other customers who came in. If it was necessary he dropped his voice or merely talked about inconsequential things.

– I'd say yes it is something you're always very conscious of in your mind. Not just workwise but all the time socially too: when are you going to get round to telling someone about being in prison and what for, how're they going to take it when you do? Whenever I possibly can I avoid it; I mean my family knows and Terry knows and you know, but so far that's all. Oh and that manager at the training place, obviously he'd have to have known because he knew I was coming there from the borstal. But I don't think the others knew, the other trainees, they were just other long-term unemployed people.

Actually there was a girl there and we got a bit friendly, we still write to each other now. Nothing serious but she was a nice girl. One day I thought Well all right I'll tell her, so I did. Not all of it, I told her I'd been in prison but I didn't say what for. She asked me what for, so I said well I'd tell her one day when we knew each other a bit better. That was how it was left. I think women like a bit of mystery in a bloke though don't they, you know what I mean?

This whether to tell people or not, it's not a problem, it's more what you might call a bit of a worry. I think when I've got a job and things I'll feel more confident about it, but just for the time being I keep myself to myself.

Yes certainly I will, I'll think about that for next time, yes.

– My dad, well I call him that but he's not really my dad, my mam only married him a couple of years back. She and my real dad are divorced and there's not very much I can tell you about him, it was a time ago, not long after I first went inside. I think that sort of sorted things out between them, they hadn't been happy quite a long time before: always rows or silences, you know what I mean? Ernie who's my stepdad, he's a nice bloke, him and me we get on a treat. I think my mam's happier with him than she was before. Like every woman she's a worrier, but a lot of women are like that aren't they? She does worry about every little thing. We get on, I mean we don't ever quarrel or anything, but sometimes I do have to sort of try to cheer her up. I'm more the sort of person who puts things out of my mind and doesn't worry about them, I tell her I don't think you should go around being depressed all the time. Obviously everyone has things get them down now and again, but my feeling is you should try not to show it.

No we never talk about that, her and me, we never have, not that it was her father I killed. I don't think we've ever looked at it that way: I never have and I don't think she does either. You know it's all in the past now, that's the way I look at it and as far as I know she looks at it the same. I mean she's never brought it up to me or anything. To tell you the truth I never give it much thought and I shouldn't think she does either.

Anyway, you asked me last time to think about how I saw things going for the future didn't you, so shall I tell you that? What I'd say about it is that I'm quite optimistic. The reason is because number one is I'm young, and that's a big point in my favour. Twenty-one's nothing in someone's whole life is it, so everything's ahead for me. I'm friendly and cheerful and easygoing and that's another good point.

What I learned in the time while I was inside was nothing. Yes I do answer a bit quick, yes. Funny, someone said that to me once at St Andrews. But my main thought now is each day that goes by it goes further and further away, I'm gradually putting prison completely behind me. I mean I'm not saying I'd forget it, because you can't obviously, not something of that sort; but you don't want to have something on your mind all the time.

Could it happen again, you mean that I did it again, killed someone else? Well that's a very nasty question isn't it? I don't mean nasty that you ask me, but a nasty thing to think about. But I know I don't need to think long about that one, because I know the answer is definitely No. No I'm sure I couldn't, quite sure: I can't see that being any kind of problem in the future. The reason I can say I'm so sure is I know myself and I've grown up you see. I wouldn't say I was fully mature or anything, but I feel I really do know myself, and I know it couldn't possibly happen again ever.

No I don't worry about it, there's no point. I've got my whole life in front of me, and I've lost a lot of time out of it. So now I want to get on with the future and make it the best sort of future that I can.

Yes I suppose it might include marriage, I don't know; I haven't given a lot of thought to it yet because I haven't had a lot of opportunity for meeting girls and things. I'd like to have a job and my own house and a car, preferably a white one. Oh and another thing I've always wanted is to have a white suit, I've always fancied a nice white suit I don't know why. What sort of job? Well what I'd most like to be in the world is a professional snooker player: Steve Davies, someone like that. Incredible he is: swish plonk, swish plonk, swisk plonk all round the table, one after another, just like that. Fantastic. And a very nice chap, so everyone says: the perfect gentleman.

Seriously? More seriously even than that d'you mean? All right, well I'll tell you. I don't think you'll think this sounds more serious, but it is. I've thought about it a lot the last year or so. What I'd really like to do is be either a policeman or a prison officer, I don't mind which. I don't agree with robbings and crimes of that sort at all, and I think it's a really decent useful job to help stop things like that happening. A lot of people have the idea people who do serious crimes such as murder are either very callous or they've got a screw loose. Well I could show them different, and that basically I'm a very honest person that people could trust and rely on. So I think if you're young and something good like that is what your aim in life is, it shows that in the future you're going to have no problem. No problem at all.

Good, yes, no, thanks to you too. It's been my pleasure.

TWO

Pretty well the whole story

EDGAR JOHNSON

An elderly white-haired man, long legged and tall, he sat in the old armchair in his council flat sitting-room, his bedroom-slippered feet stretched out towards the small coal fire in the grate. From time to time he rolled up a needle-thin cigarette between his fingers, from the tobacco tin on his lap. Gold-rimmed spectacles, pale blue eyes, his voice soft and quiet; often there were long silences as he frowned and tried to order his thoughts.

– Course you'll understand for an old man seventy-eight going on seventy-nine, and it all having taken place such a long time ago and everything – well it's not easy for me to remember every little detail in every instance of what took place. The exact order of things and so on, my memory's very bad now for dates. As you get older you find you can't remember something that only happened only last year, or even only last week sometimes you know. It's a funny thing the human mind is, it plays tricks on you: you'll remember one thing with absolute clarity, every single detail of it, and yet there's no reason why you should, it's not all that specially important. Yet another thing, when it really would be a help to you, you can hardly recall anything about it at all.

I've been out of prison now fifteen years. That would make it at the time I came out I'd be fifty-four or somewhere around that age. No wait a minute, what am I saying? I wasn't fifty-four, I was sixty-four: now that's straight away an example of what I was telling you about, immediately getting things wrong and all mixed up. Now then: if I was sixty-four when I came out of prison, and I'd done twelve years inside, that means I was fifty-two when I went into prison, or somewhere around there, I can't quite remember exactly. I'd never been in prison before for anything, and I've never been back again in prison since: I've had only that one sentence that's all.

I couldn't tell you exactly when I was born. My birth certificate's somewhere in one of those old boxes up there on top of the wardrobe. It's quite a while now since I have had any occasion to use it, I could look it out for you though if you wish. No as you say it doesn't really matter. At a guess I'd say I would have been born 1910 or 1912, somewhere about then. And as to where I was born, I can't tell you that either: it was only a tiny little village of a place in the middle of Norfolk, getting on towards King's Lynn area or near there. I seem to remember as a child King's Lynn was the nearest big place of any size: it was always a bit of an event to go to King's Lynn. I remember a time or two when I was very young going there with my brothers and sisters in my father's horse and cart he borrowed from the farm where he worked.

He was just an ordinary farm labourer, and we all lived in one of those cottages that the farmer had for his workers, tied cottages they called them because they were tied to the job. If you lost your job you lost your home as well. I don't remember how often that happened to us, but I know it must have. Twice or three times I think, because I remember different places we were in, even if I couldn't now tell you their names.

I'm afraid I definitely can't tell you that at all, how many brothers and sisters I had. I was the first one, the eldest; and I always used to think it was because of that that I had the hardest time. More was expected of me, in the way of fetching and carrying things, or peeling potatoes, or going errands and so on. That was the reason I left home at an early age when I was about twelve, or thirteen at the most. It wasn't so much I was unhappy, my parents weren't cruel or beat me, nothing like that; but I never seemed to have a fair chance of a life of my own. There was always so little money in the house, and I was expected to go out and do odd jobs for other people. Then what money I got for it, I had to bring it all home and give it to my mother to help feed and clothe the others. I remember feeling I'd never have anything of my own in my life if I didn't stand up for myself. So one day I told my parents I was going to set out in life on my own. I don't remember them being particularly upset about it, they must have had perhaps five or six others to look after by then, so probably they looked on it it'd be one less mouth to feed. I wanted my own independence, that would be a good way to express it, yes.

I went to Grantham in Lincolnshire to start with, then I moved on up into Yorkshire. It was in Yorkshire that one way or another I've since spent most of the rest of my life, till these last few years when I've been living in the south here in Portsmouth. It must sound as though I've been something of a roving stone, I suppose in some ways it's true, I have. But there've been fairly long periods as well when I stayed in one place. I couldn't say wherever I got before long I was wanting to move on somewhere else: that's just been the way it's turned out, that's all.

As to what my very first job was after I left home, I couldn't quite tell you what it was, I'm sure. It'd be farm work of some kind, that I can say: it was the only kind of work I knew, and I was a tall healthy lad, and strong. Certainly I wasn't one not used to working hard, and for long hours too, I've always been like that. I might not have had much in the way of schooling, but I never had trouble finding work. I think I probably did mostly picking and harvesting, depending on the season. Another thing I could do, was I was quite handy with machinery. I've always been what's called mechanically minded. If a tractor or a van or something broke down, I could usually fix it up again without it having to be laid up at a garage somewhere out of action. That was a very useful ability to have was that one: there were times I'd go into a farmyard and there was some broken piece of machinery or other, and I'd tell them I'd mend it for them. When I did they'd often think I was a useful lad to have around the place and they'd keep me on

then for a while. I used to ask them for my food, to sleep in
the barn or somewhere, and just a bit of pocket money.

In my time, till well into my twenties it would be, I did
nearly every sort of job you could think of. Gardener at a big
hotel on the coast near Scarborough was one I remember;
garage mechanic, I think it was in Hull; on the fishing boats
a time or two, but I didn't much care for that; furniture van
driver; a whole number of things. All that was important to
me was it had to be outdoor work: I never could stand the
idea of being in an office or a shop or something of that sort.
Another thing I didn't like much was towns either. I was a
born and bred country boy, and what I liked was being
outside in the fresh air, not having the sort of job I was tied
down at.

It was the same with the ladies. I seemed to have an eye
for them, and they in return, they very often seemed to have
an eye for me. I think to most of them I was a good looking
young man and always ready for a bit of romance. Well it
was true, I was: and it wasn't something I found it much
difficult to come by ever either. I liked girls' company,
especially if they were pretty; I preferred female company
much more than that of men's. I can look back now on some
very happy times I had with girls and young ladies, I can
indeed. But of course I can also look back on some very
unhappy times with women later in my life too. Still that's
another story which I'll tell you about in due course.

Then, at this time I'm talking about when I was in my
twenties and so on, there was a lot of pleasure; just so long
as one thing remained how I wanted it. That was that I
would never let it get too serious. I always used to make that
quite clear right at the beginning. Very often it'd come a
time, it seemed almost inevitably it would, when questions
like settling down, or even marriage, would come into the
conversation. From their side of course, not from mine; and
as soon as it did, that was it, I was off like a flash. I had this
big fear of getting caught, getting trapped by somebody as
you might say. And it wasn't just for my sake, but for theirs
too: I knew I'd got what they call a roving eye, and I knew

from experience quite a lot of women had too. So the way I saw it, I might marry someone and settle down with her, but then it was bound to happen before long that I'd get involved with somebody else. It was bound to, there was just no way it couldn't happen; and no married woman's going to be prepared to put up with that sort of thing. I always knew that; and in the end, well that's just exactly what did happen you know.

I find I do get tired a bit easily these days, you know my voice starts to go. Shall we stop there for today and I'll make us a nice cup of tea?

– Marriage has always been something I wanted to try and avoid, but we all have these good intentions and then don't stick by them. In the end, when I did get married, I can't exactly remember how old I was, but I'd think I was perhaps twenty-eight or twenty-nine. And it turned out just exactly as I'd thought it would, and it didn't work. My wife was called Kathleen: she was quite a bit younger than me, not much more than twenty I think she was, and very immature. She'd no idea what she wanted in life at all. She told me all she wanted was me. So in the end I agreed to it, and we got married. It was a very big mistake altogether it was, because I think it can only have been about two years or so and then we drifted apart.

By that time the war had started, and I thought as a single man, or at least the equivalent of one because although we weren't divorced we were separated, I thought I'd be called up. But I was working in, well it wasn't so much a factory as a big kind of a repair depot for Army vehicles. And that was essential war work so I didn't have to go for the Army. My skills with trucks and lorries and things of that sort, I suppose that was far more use than marching around as a soldier. So I stayed in that occupation all the way through the war. About the only snag to it was I had all the time to stay in that one place, the depot, which was just outside Leeds.

Then at the end of the war I got married for a second time. My wife's name was Joan. As a matter of fact she was the reason why my first marriage broke up. She'd been a friend of my first wife, Kathleen's, and it was through her that we met. Before long we'd taken quite a fancy to each other, and that was what upset Kathleen and made her leave me. Joan and I didn't get married at first because we couldn't, I wasn't divorced: we just lived together, more or less that way all through the war, and then when it ended I got my divorce and we married. She wasn't in the forces in the war, Joan; but she did some kind of war work or other, I don't exactly remember what. But it made it that we weren't always together; I think myself in a kind of a way, that's what probably kept us together such a long time.

But then when the war finished and her job finished and mine did too, as I say it was that that made us decide on a permanent marriage, which is what we did. We'd both of us got a little money saved up, not much but enough, and we bought a small garage and petrol station with its own house attached. I think it was getting on towards Whitby way or somewhere round there. But it was in rather an isolated sort of place on a crossroads near a village. We made a bad mistake, because it simply wasn't profitable at all. Petrol was still rationed from after the war and the sales of it were very restricted; and it was the kind of a place not many people'd bring their cars out to for repair. If there was something wrong they'd more likely have it done in town where they could collect it easier.

The other thing that went wrong as much or even more so, was that being there every day Joan got very lonely, and she also started to get very suspicious and jealous as well. There'd only need to be a young lady driver would come in for petrol or because there was something wrong with her car: we'd start talking and perhaps have a joke about something, and Joan would be watching it all from the kitchen window. Then as soon as the young woman had gone, there'd be an almighty row about it. And if that same young woman happened to come to the garage again for something else the following week, well you can imagine what accusations were flying around. There'd be nothing to it, it was all perfectly innocent from beginning to end, but Joan never saw it that way.

Well you know that was no situation for people to be married to each other in was it? It couldn't continue like that, and so one night we sat down and had a talk about it. We didn't have children to consider or anything, and we decided the best thing would be if we separated and went our own ways: sell up the house and business that we were continually losing money on, and divide up what there was left. It was amiable. She decided she was going to go back and live over the other side of Leeds with her mother, and I was going to set off on my travels again, and wander wherever the fancy took me.

So that was what we did, and I'm not sure now how many years it was for; but it was for quite a good few years, I do remember that. As far as I was concerned everything went along smoothly, I never had difficulty getting work, and I lived mostly in digs or boarding houses. There was one time I remember I was a crane operator on a building site: that was very good money and another time I worked in an open cast mine; I did any number of things. If I liked a job and the wages were right I stayed, and if I didn't and they weren't, I moved on.

Joan and I had agreed that there was no need to get divorced, both of us were sure we'd not want to get married again to someone else. We left it though that if either of us ever did, the other one would agree to divorce straight away. And that's how it went on for quite a while, and we weren't even in touch with each other. Then one day, I can't exactly remember now where it was I was working, I think it might have been when I was at an agricultural machinery firm; but then, blow me, she suddenly turned up there and asked me could we meet and have a talk when I'd finished work.

My first thought about it was she'd come to ask me if we could have a divorce so she could get married to somebody.

But no not a bit of it: it wasn't that at all, what she'd come to say was she missed me, she didn't like living without me, and could we get back together again and give it another try. You could have knocked me down with a feather.

You know, if I'd been sensible of course I'd have told her there and then it was a completely silly idea and one that couldn't possibly work. But I didn't want to hurt her feelings by saying it just like that: so I said what I'd do was think about it, and we arranged we'd have another talk a few days after. She said all right, she'd come back. She said what she was offering me was she'd got quite a nice house of her own she'd bought; and that her brother had started up a long-distance haulage business of his own a few years back, it was going well and he was ready and willing to offer me a job there.

Well it just happened to be at that time that I was not very happy at the agricultural machinery place. So I thought it all over, but when we had our next meeting I was still a good bit doubtful about it all. She could see I was hesitating, but women have a way of doing these things, and in the finish I let her talk me into it.

Oh dear me it was, it really was a very serious mistake, the worst I ever made in the whole of my life. I moved to live in her house, and the first thing I had to put up with was the rest of her family, except the one brother who gave me the job. They were all antagonistic to me. They'd been antagonistic ever since I'd met her: first because I lived with her without marrying her, then when I did marry her they all tried to argue her out of it, and finally when we separated then they'd no more time for me whatsoever. So when we went back together again they ignored us completely then. I think Joan went now and again to her mother's; but when she came home I could always tell where she'd been, because she always started all the suspicion and jealousy business again.

It went on and on, and it got worse and worse. There were times when she'd even start quarrelling in broad day-light in the street with me, shouting at me and hitting me

with her fists. If I just said a polite word to some woman I
knew slightly in a shop, or had a little laugh with a waitress
in a café or something of that sort: it was exactly like it'd
been before, one after another rows rows rows.

To make matters worse, we'd only been back together
less than a year I should think, and then her brother took ill,
the one that I was working for. He had a very serious illness
which they thought he was going to die from, and he had to
go into hospital for weeks, in fact I'm not exactly sure it
wasn't two or three months in the end. I was left having to
run the haulage business, and that meant working very long
hours and sometimes even having to stay away from home.
And another thing was that my brother-in-law's wife, her
name was Rita, she had to go to the hospital every night to
visit him, so sometimes to help her out I took her there in
the car or a van.

Well of course it wasn't long was it before Joan started
getting the idea there was something going on between us.
There was one occasion I remember when she saw a new
nightie or some undies or something on the washing line
when she was walking past her house, and she accused me
of buying them for her. And another time, well this was my
own fault really: it was a stupid thing to say but I was
teasing Joan and I said Rita was better than she was in bed.

So things were getting to be very bad again and this is
where we come now to the night in question when it all
happened. This is nearly thirty years ago now of course, and
my memory's not clear about every little detail of it though,
you know. Joan and me, we'd been having another of our
almost daily rows; and I think it was about July time and a
nice evening. One of the ideas we'd been considering now
and again between us was moving to live in another house,
somewhere that was not so near to her parents. There was
one we'd had our eye on right up on the moors; and I
suggested to give us both a break, why didn't we drive out
there on this particular evening and have another look at it.
I had a van of my own that I used at work, and we decided
to go for the drive in that.

We went up towards the moors along a quiet winding country road that we knew, a sort of back road, and at one point it ran along round a sort of cliff edge, like a ravine with some woods down below it. Just as we happened to be getting near to that part, all of a sudden Joan started going for me about Rita again: she had her handbag in her hand and she started to hit me with it. I sort of put my arm up like that, you see, to protect myself; and I can't quite exactly remember now whether I did give her a little push backwards or not. And this van you see, it didn't have doors that opened outwards, it had those sliding doors that go backwards and forwards like this, and it had a bench seat as well, not the usual ordinary type of passenger seats. I don't know if you know the sort of thing, but sometimes what they very often do those doors, especially if they're old, is they quite often slide backwards and forwards while you're driving. So you see in this case, that was just more or less exactly what happened: at the very moment I gave her the little push, the door had flown open and she went backwards out of it. Out of the van, over the edge of the road, and all the way down the cliff into a wood at the bottom of it.

Naturally I stopped the van as soon as I safely could, and went back and climbed all the way down the cliff to find her. When I did, I could see she was badly hurt: she wasn't breathing or anything, though I didn't know whether she was dead or not. I carried her up and then I laid her down on the roadside just at the back of my van. At that very moment someone came along in a car, and stopped and said could he help; so I asked him please would he drive on to the next house he came to, and would he phone for help from there because there'd been an accident. I'm not sure now how long it was before the ambulance came, and then they took her off to the hospital. I didn't go with them because I wasn't sure what I should do really. I thought the best thing perhaps would be if I went to her brother's house where my sister-in-law was, and I told her what had happened. A little while later the police came: they confirmed to me she was dead, but they didn't ask me questions or anything, just said they wanted to take my van away for examination.

I stayed that night at my sister-in-law's, and the next day I thought I'd better go and see a solicitor, which I did. On his advice, I didn't go to my wife's funeral, on account of all her relatives' antagonistic feelings towards me. It was only a few days afterwards, and I think it was later the same day, or it might have been the next morning I can't quite remember now, by arrangement the police came to the solicitor's office and took a statement from me, and then they arrested me and charged me with her murder.

That's about as far as I can go again today, so shall we continue tomorrow? Any time from about two o'clock onwards, if that's all right for you?

A small middle-aged woman in bright green trousers and a short black winter coat appeared unexpectedly in the middle of our conversation next afternoon. She had let herself in through the front door, and then came into the room and stopped. She stood swaying slightly unsteadily and blinking. 'I'm Sandra' she said, slurring her words a little: 'Sandra's my name, I'm pleased to make your acquaintance.'

Edgar stood up unhurriedly and took her by the hand. 'I think you'd better lie down dear and have a little nap for a while' he said gently. 'Come along now.' He led her out.

– She's just a neighbour who comes in sometimes, she'll not disturb us.

Well yesterday I was telling you how I was arrested wasn't I? Well after they'd charged me the police took me off to prison on remand in custody to await trial. I forget how long it was, about several months I know, and it was summer and very hot. Not many people came to see me: my sister-in-law once I think, but not anyone else. Then eventually, either just before Christmas or shortly afterwards I think it was, I was taken to court for my trial. I was sure I'd get off; but the police exaggerated everything, they made it

all sound very black indeed. They said I'd planned it all
very carefully, and what I'd done was I'd hit her over the
head with something, I'd fixed the door to make it look like
it wouldn't fasten properly, and I'd pushed her out of the
van at the edge of the cliff so it'd seem she'd fallen out by
accident. And they said that I climbed down and brought
her back up to the top, and laid her down behind the rear
wheel of the van, and I was just going to back it over her
head when this man in the car came along.

It was absurd, it was all absolutely absurd. The police
produced witnesses to say they knew we quarrelled a lot,
and there was no one at all on my side, not one single
person. A different counsel might have done better for me;
and the Judge, he was the worst one of the lot. He kept
joining in all the time when I was being cross questioned,
and he even interrupted my barrister when he was trying to
bring out points in my favour. The trial lasted I think it was
about three days as I remember; and I was found guilty, and
before he sentenced me the Judge said 'The jury have seen
through your cunning.'

So there it was, I was sentenced to life imprisonment: and
I can tell you, I felt very very bitter about it. I had it in my
mind that I would appeal, yes, to see if I couldn't get it
reduced to accidental death, manslaughter at least or something of that sort. But when I talked it over with my
solicitor he said he didn't think there was any hope at all
unless we could produce some new witnesses, which I
couldn't. My sister-in-law Rita came to see me once or
twice, and she said she thought the best thing would be for
me to do my sentence. I expected it would probably be
about seven years or possibly eight years at the very most,
and we thought we'd then think about making a fresh start.
But what I did in the end was ten years and by that time
we'd more or less lost contact with each other. I was no
trouble to anybody in prison, I kept myself to myself: I
think at different times I was in Armley in Leeds, then
Hull, Leicester, and then down here to Portsmouth from
where I got my discharge.

Did I say twelve years to you originally? Yes well it's right it was twelve, I did ten and then another two on top. Only what I call the two years on top, that was actually what's called a recall. As I expect you'll know, when you come out from a life sentence you're not free of it, you're only let out when they decide you should be; and then it's on licence to a probation officer and under his supervision all the time. And I believe it was Lincoln I first came out from after the ten years. When I did I was under the supervision of a very young probation officer, he wasn't much more than a lad really. As far as I could tell he'd never had a life sentence prisoner to supervise before, his only experience had been dealing with young boys. He gave me the impression he was frightened with my case, out of his depth altogether and had no idea how to handle it.

I was perfectly all right when I came out, but it does take you time to settle down you know, after a long sentence. I didn't drink or things like that, and after a few weeks I'd got myself a job of some sort or other. Then I met a lady and I'd nowhere to live, so I moved in on a temporary basis with her. We had one or two quarrels, nothing serious, they were no more than tiffs that's all: but this probation officer, he found out about them and said I'd knocked her about and what does he do but he has me taken back to prison again. I mean it was ridiculous you know, he completely overreacted. But there you are, you can be taken back into prison again just on their say-so, and that's what happened to me. I'd only been out two or three months, I can't exactly remember, it may have been a bit more: but I was back inside and it was another two years after that before they decided to let me out again.

Being in a way used to prison by then like I was, I didn't like going back again but I didn't find it all so that much of a terrible shock. All the same I was very glad when they told me they were ready to let me have another try. By then I'd been sent down to prison here in Portsmouth: I came out from here and this is where I've stayed ever since. And it's been fifteen years I've been free now, and everything's gone

ahead perfectly smoothly. At the moment I've got a very
nice young probation officer, Ian, who supervises me: he's
been looking after me for five or six years or possibly a bit
longer, I couldn't tell you exactly. And previous to him
there was another good one, a man called Mr Drake. He was
very very good.

So now prison's just a bad memory in the distant past for
me. The thing that's most helped to wipe it completely out
of my mind has been that when I finally came out, I was
lucky that not long after my release, about four years or so, I
met a lady whose name was Grace. She would be at that
time fifty-five perhaps or fifty-six, and she was a widowed
lady whose husband had passed on a few years before. We
just seemed to click together immediately, just like that. So
after a very short time we got married.

I never actually met them, but I believe she had I think it
was two grown-up children, who were married and lived up
north, Manchester or somewhere that way.

Grace and I, we had eight very happy years together, we
really did. She was about the gentlest kindest person anyone
could ever hope to meet. Once or twice I did feel I ought to
tell her something about myself, my past and all the rest of
it: but the funny thing was you know, she never wanted to
know. I tried a time or two, I remember I said to her 'Grace
you know, you don't really know anything about me at all.'
But she always used to say to me 'Edgar' she said, 'I don't
want to know anything about what's in the past, I'm just so
happy like we are that I don't want anything in the world to
spoil it.' She died it'll be two years ago next month now.
I've often thought in my own mind that perhaps she knew,
you know, that she'd got that illness which she had and she
knew she was going to die from it, and she wanted to make
the most out of what time she had left. She was a very kind
person: this was her flat and this is all her furniture, and we
lived here all those years and then when she passed away, I
stayed on.

I can't see myself getting married any more times, no.
That young woman who came earlier on that you met,

Sandra, well she's no more than just a friend really, she's only here temporarily. She had a couple of rooms in those old houses you've probably noticed down at the bottom of the road that're being demolished: they belong to the council, and when they find her somewhere else to live I expect she'll move on. I said to her she could stay for a while if she wanted to; I expect you noticed she does have one or two problems, she takes a bit too much drink now and again. She's a nice person though, and I'd say more than anything else what she needs is someone to look after her.

She knows nothing about my past, and she's another one who's never seemed as if she wanted to. She doesn't know who you are or why you come here: I've told her you're talking to me about my war memories for a book you're going to write, and that you prefer it better if we talk on our own. By the way if you should happen to see Ian my probation officer any time, I'd be glad if you'd not mention her to him. It might only lead to questions and things, and I wouldn't want to upset her.

So then there we are, that's the end of everything there is to tell you about myself, unless there's anything more you want to know that you can think of. There's nothing else that I can remember: I think what I've said is pretty well the whole story.

It obviously wasn't. After a carefully gradual lessening in the strictness of supervision, in most cases after about four years, a probation officer is thinking of asking the Home Office's permission to suspend most of the conditions of a lifer's licence. It was most unusual to learn that almost fifteen years after his release Edgar Johnson was still under active supervision.

I asked him if I could go back and see him the following week for a further talk.

— Yes well funnily enough I was only thinking that myself you know, how somehow it had never seemed to come up. You're perfectly right, it is unusual for someone still to be seeing his probation officer as long after release as I've been doing, normally yes it's more like for four years or so. Mind you I'm not complaining about it, not in any way at all. I'm perfectly happy to go on seeing Ian every month or two like I do, or anyone else for that matter, perfectly happy. In fact you know to be honest with you I think myself I'd prefer it to go on that way for good. Then I've got the feeling there's always someone I can talk to if I want to, they'll help me along as it were.

What it was you see is that now and again – and it is only now and again mark you – well there have been one or two little what you might call little scrapes or bits of bother. Nothing very serious at all; but all the same, when you're a life sentence prisoner on licence, you're very vulnerable you see, to the slightest sort of thing of any kind. It having once got as far as me being recalled to prison after I'd come out, well it's only natural things sometimes can look to be more serious than they actually are. The first time it was all really a lot of fuss about nothing, but you can see how perhaps the police felt about it.

I'd been out I suppose after my recall about three years, or it might have been four, I can't quite properly remember. There was this young woman I knew, she lived over the other side of the city somewhere, and for a time we were quite friendly. What I didn't know though you see, was that before I came on the scene she'd had a boyfriend, and he was a black man. One evening I was just coming back to her flat, and I heard this terrible shouting and screaming going on inside. So I opened the door, and there was this black man I'd never seen before in my life, and from what I could see of it just on the spur of the moment, it really did look to me like he was going to attack her. There was a bottle, I think it was a beer bottle or something of that sort on the table, and I went to pick it up and defend her with it. Then he sort of made a lunge at me and I dropped it, and the bottle broke. I picked it up again, and then he made another sort of lunge at me you see, and the bottle just grazed his face. It wasn't anything serious, only a few little scratches, nothing that could have really hurt him. But this girl was still shouting and screaming and somebody called the police: and in the end what it came down to was I was taken to court, and I was charged with malicious wounding would you believe.

It was completely exaggerated out of all proportion, but of course me being a life-sentence prisoner out on licence, I was in a very exposed and dangerous position indeed. Well that Mr Drake I was telling you of, the probation officer who was so good, he made a big plea to the court about me trying to start my life all over again. In the end he managed to get them to be sensible about it, and they told me they weren't going to send me back to prison, instead they'd give me another chance so all I got was bound over for it.

That was the first one. And I think strictly speaking the rule is that you're supposed to be entirely free of trouble of any kind whatsoever for four complete years before they'll consider you having your licence conditions slackened a bit. For me you see, up till then had only been three, so that meant they had to be thinking then of another four clear years.

Then the second event was very very unfortunate indeed, that was all that was. This would be just about four years afterwards exactly or perhaps a little more, I don't remember now. Another young woman I started having an association with, it was nothing serious and it hadn't been going on very long, but one night she and I had a row about something trivial or other, and she ran out of the flat where I was living at the time. I'd no idea where she was going, I thought it might be perhaps to her sister who lived further down somewhere. But to my amazement the next thing I knew the police were banging at the door.

They came in, and they started searching the flat. They wouldn't tell me what they were looking for, they never do; but then one of them came back in the room with something in his hand, and he said 'What's this?' All it was was an air pistol sort of a thing, but not a big one or new one: it was one I'd bought in the market one day about six months earlier, I'd thought one of my young nephews might like it for Christmas or a birthday present. I'd put it away in a drawer or in the bedroom cupboard I think, and I'd forgotten all about it, I didn't even remember it was there. And this girl after we'd had this row, it can only have been out of pure spite that's all, but she'd gone round to the police and told them I'd got a gun and I'd threatened her with it. It was completely untrue, absolutely and completely.

Of course the police knew, but she didn't, that I was a lifer on licence; and of course when you are, one of your conditions is you're not supposed to have guns or knives, or weapons of any kind. It was hardly what you could call a weapon, it couldn't possibly have done any harm to anyone even if you could have aimed it straight. All the same, there it was: I was back to court again and I think that time it was threatening behaviour I was charged with. I don't quite remember the exact nature of it. By then Ian had come on the scene, he was my probation officer, and he was the one who came and spoke in court for me. He said I was an old man getting on, which I was, and he did feel there was really a good chance I was settling down. I remember he said it would be very very sad indeed if I was to be put back in prison again at my age. I think he said as well that he would offer continuing close supervision of me, I think those were his words.

So that's how it's stayed since, I only have to see him about every three months or so. And so far at least I don't think I've given him any cause to regret what he said.

Shall I make us a nice cup of tea?

THREE

Tears don't count though do they?

CAROL BOWEN

Askham Grange, formerly a Victorian manor house, is an open prison for women a few miles outside York. It has open gates, a short entrance driveway, and a tree-lined duck pond. The prisoners' dormitories and work rooms are round the back. Inside the front building are the administration offices, and long parquet-floored corridors. Down at the end of one of them is a high-ceilinged wood-panelled room with heavy polished tables and leather-seated chairs, occasionally used for staff meetings but more usually deserted.

She sat on a faded brocade-upholstered settee beneath the window: short, sturdily built, fair haired and brown eyed, her small voice sometimes somehow echoing.

— I'm very shy, you mightn't think it but I am. Talking sitting here's all right, but if we were outside I'd be frightened, all nervous, my fingers trembling and couldn't speak properly, my voice'd be so tight in my throat. One of the officers took me out in her car a few weeks ago, we went into York and looked at the shops and things and had a cup of tea in a snack bar. I was sure everyone was looking at me, I thought everyone'd know where I'd come from. Jean, Mrs Read, that's the officer, she said everyone felt like that the first time they went out. I'm worried because my daughter's coming to see me in two weeks with her boyfriend. It'd be awful if I made an exhibition of myself because I was too shy to talk properly. It's ridiculous with someone my age.

I'm forty-one unfortunately. Well I say unfortunately because it's the best years of a woman's life isn't it, between thirty and forty: gone for me and I'll never get them back. More than ten years wasted in prison. Oh well perhaps I'm not too old to start again when I get out; that'll be a year from January. See if I can't do better for myself, start at the beginning again eh? I've no idea doing what: I hope I'll get a job waitressing or a barmaid or something. I'm not an ambitious person; I'm not a very clever one either, so there won't be a lot of scope. I might get married again mightn't I? That'd be a laugh wouldn't it? Not seriously no, I'm just joking: that's one thing I'm absolutely certain of, that is. No more men for me, I've had enough of men. I'll never make a fool of myself that way any more, that's one thing that's sure.

– I was born in Birmingham and adopted soon after, when I was three weeks, I think. I don't know the circumstances at all. One thing I've never had is the feeling some people do, that they get to a certain age and then they want to find out about themselves and who their parents were. It's never worked like that for me. As far as I was concerned, the people who brought me up were my parents, especially my mum as I called her. I still think of her as that, she was the only mother I had. She was a very lovely person, I remember her with real love and affection. She had long wavy brown hair and brown eyes, and was always cuddling me and playing with me. She always seemed to be laughing and smiling all the time.

There you are though, things happen don't they, and when I was seven she died. I don't know what of, I remember she had to go into hospital very quickly and she only lived for about a week. I was sent to my grandmother's to live, that was my mother's mother. She had other children and they were a lot older than me, they were like aunties. There's not much else I remember about them. She must have been a good woman to take me in, but none of that period made much impression on me. Perhaps I was too sad to think of anything much else except how I missed my mother and wished she could come back again. They're like that aren't they children, things happen around them but they never properly know what's going on?

How long I was at my grandmother's I've no idea. My

feeling is when I look back on it that it can't have been long. I think it might have been about a year. What I do remember is my father, the man I called my father that is, coming to my grandmother's house and telling me that he'd got a new house and I was going to go and live with him again. And the other thing he told me was I'd got a new mother and sister, and we were all going to live as one family.

It was in Bristol, he'd got a job there. And he'd got a new wife; or I think she was his wife, they might only have been living together at first. My recollection of her is she was quite a bit older than my mother had been. That might have been because she was a much less cheerful and jolly person though. Her name was Shirley. Right from the beginning I hated her and she hated me. She had her own daughter whose name was Lucy. She was older than me, about twelve when I first went there. We didn't take to each other either.

I was told there was going to be no difference between us; and I was told as well that I was to call Shirley my mother. I wouldn't do it because she wasn't: to me my mother had died and nobody would replace her. When you grow up and look back you see things in a different light a bit; and I can see now I didn't make things very easy for Shirley. All the same she wasn't very nice to me either: she never tried very hard to understand me, or why I was cheeky or disobedient. She was very houseproud too: the slightest thing left untidy or out of place, she'd slap me on the legs. And I was sent to bed without any tea if I came home late from school, or because I left dirty clothes in the bathroom, things like that. She was quick tempered and so was I, we used to have some real shouting matches. Once I stuck my tongue out at her, and she ran off and got a spoon with mustard on it and covered my tongue with it. And another time I swore at her, I was really angry, I told her I'd fucking kill her. She set about me with her fists that time, I think I had to stay in my bedroom two whole days. My father always backed her up, I don't suppose he could do anything else when you look at it. Lucy never stood up for me either, and she was always telling her mother tales. She'd say I'd done things she'd done herself, that she was trying to avoid getting into trouble for.

I wasn't good at school and I was always truanting too, so that was another thing I was regularly punished for. By the time I was eleven things had got to the point when Shirley and my father said they couldn't keep me under control any longer. When I stayed out all night one night with a girl from my class in school, that was finally it. We hadn't done anything terrible, only slept in an old shed we knew of in someone's garden: it was for the adventure and nothing happened. But they got the local children's people to come and see me: the woman was very nice about it I remember, she asked me would I sooner live in a children's home outside Bristol. I said yes I would, I'd much sooner, so that was where I went. I was nine I think then; no ten.

I was much happier there; and the house mother was really nice. There were about fourteen children there altogether, with ages from very young who were not much more than babies, right up to I think about fifteen. I really liked it, specially when they let me help with bathing the young ones and giving them their teas. I had a particular friend who was one of the older girls, her name was Peggy and she was supposed to be a bad lot, but I liked her. She was fourteen, and to me she seemed to be very adventurous and grown up. Once a week I was allowed to go to my parents' house for tea, and one time they told me they were going on their holidays for two weeks, so they wouldn't be able to have me the next weekend. When I told Peggy she said why didn't we go to the house while they were away, and break in and see if there was anything we could pinch there like money or jewellery. That's what we did, we broke in the following Saturday afternoon and stole some rings and a clock, then we took them to a shop Peggy knew which bought things second-hand. We'd no idea of the value of what we'd taken but it was worth a lot more than we got for it. Only some neighbours had seen us breaking into the house and had told the police.

Peggy and I took off for Weston-super-Mare. We spent

two days there wandering round an amusement park place, and we slept in one of the shelters up at the far end of the promenade. Then the police picked us up. As a result I was sent to an approved school in the Midlands. It wasn't bad, it was more or less completely open like this place is: like a girls' boarding school really, and you could go out without supervision so long as you were back at what time they said.

I absconded from there twice, once for six weeks and the second time for ten, so after that I was kept in what they called one of the closed blocks. The first time I went, I stayed with a girl in London who'd been in the approved school herself and been discharged a few weeks before. She was living with a man in Clapham in a flat and they put me up. In the end I went back myself voluntarily to the approved school and gave myself up. The first time they let me have less freedom, but I wasn't locked in completely; that's why I was able to go on the run again the second time.

At the flat in Clapham, the girl who was there went out on Sunday all day, I think to see her mother in north London somewhere. So the chap she was living with, he took me in bed with him and broke me in. I was eleven; I'd always been told it hurt the first time, but it didn't. When I absconded the second time I went to an Italian man in Blackheath, and we shared a room in a house he had that he let out in furnished rooms. I told him I was older than I was, and he was a nice man and he treated me well; I did housekeeping for him and cleaning, and cooking him some meals.

He was the first man I actually lived with. Since then there've been quite a few others if you add them up, quite a few. But they've mostly lasted a good while, two or three years: if I'm living with a man I don't go with any other man during that time, I've always been fair about that. I'm not a prostitute, I never have been: I only go with men I like, and if they want me to stay with them and look after them I'm willing to do that, or I was. One of the welfare people at Holloway when I was on remand, she said what I really was was a professional common-law wife, and I'd say that's true. If someone gave me love and affection and was nice to me,

I'd keep house for them and they could always have sex in return whenever they liked.

Then not the Italian man but a man I met when I came out from approved school, I lived nearly two years with him. I had a baby by him when I was seventeen, she was a little girl. Her name was Stella, which means 'star'. I gave her for adoption when she was three weeks old, and I've never seen her or known anything about her ever since.

She's the one coming to see me in two weeks. She'll be twenty-three now. What happened was a couple of months ago I had a letter to say she'd been trying to trace me and asking me would I agree to her being told my name and where I was? I thought well she's grown up, and I'd like to see her if she'd like to see me, so I said Yes. I thought I might not hear any more, but she wrote last month and said she'd come to visit me with her boyfriend.

I expect I'll be very shy; but it's not been too bad talking today, perhaps that'll be a help for me. Keep our fingers crossed eh?

– After my baby Stella was born, her father said he didn't want to know, he didn't want to have any more to do with me. I think the next man after him was an American soldier at one of those bases in East Anglia. He was either a lieutenant or a captain; I met him in a pub one night and he was very lonely like a lot of those Americans are. He was married and he had a couple of kids too: he was very proud of them, he used to show me their photographs. His wife hadn't come over to England with him, I think they were separated before he came here. His home was somewhere in the south, I believe he said Missouri or somewhere like that. At the beginning he used to tell me he was going to get divorce papers and everything, we'd get married and then he'd take me back to America and we'd start a new life together.

It was the usual story, you hear a lot of it between Americans and British girls eh? I didn't ever believe what he said. But I didn't mind about it: I think perhaps he almost sometimes believed it himself. And it made no difference, I'd have lived with him promises or no promises. So long as he was kind and treated me decently, which he always did. We were together perhaps two years almost, then one night he said he had to be honest with me, he'd met someone else and she was an American like he was, and he thought they were more suited to each other.

I must admit after that I did have a period when I was unsettled for a while. I started to be almost a drifter. I got one or two jobs like packing electric light bulbs in a factory in north London, working in a factory making radio parts, and some casual work waitressing. I was still sometimes going with men, but never walking the streets or being a call girl: I wasn't one for money and a good time or things of that sort. What I wanted most was friendship, companionship, somebody to be with; and I was quite happy if I was just sitting watching the television or cooking and ironing, I wasn't wanting to be taken out to expensive restaurants or clubs. I went on like that for quite a few years altogether, through most of my twenties. Sometimes there was a man and we'd settle down living together for a while. I'd start thinking perhaps this was it, it might even come to marriage one day; then that'd go on for a few months, then he'd be off with someone else. So I'd have a few months on my own until another lonely man came along, then I'd go through it all again.

I've never really known what it was about me. I was always faithful, I'm a good cook, I was never argumentative and I kept a nice clean home. I'm a Virgo and they're supposed to be neat and clean and tidy always, aren't they? But I just never seemed to have any luck with men at all. Sometimes I've thought back on it, and I've thought was it I was so boring and ordinary and unexciting? I don't think I was ever much good in bed either, so perhaps that had something to do with it, I mean I suppose that's very important to a man.

Eventually I finished up curiously enough back in Bristol.

My father and stepmother weren't living there any more, but I had an auntie I used to go and see, a sister of the one I looked on as my mother. She'd had a bit of a rough time herself one way and another, divorced and remarried and the rest of it; and she and the new man she married were in the restaurant business, a restaurant and club. They offered me a job waitressing and barmaiding for them, so I took it.

By then I was coming up to thirty; and I have to say it because it's true, to be honest I was drinking too much. Not spirits or beer, that thing called barley wine, which is a drink that's quite strong. I wasn't an incapable alcoholic, but I've thought about it since and I think I was heading that way. My auntie was more tolerant than a lot of employers would have been about late time-keeping and so on. In one sense I was fortunate there, but in another someone more strict might have pulled me up.

Altogether I wasn't living a good life though. I had a furnished room where the restaurant was, but I was spending too much time round the different pubs in the town. I didn't have a steady man friend and that might have made a difference if I had. But I was getting less particular than I had been, I have to be honest and say that as well. I met up with a Danish man off one of the boats that used to come in, and he was the nearest I had to a man friend. But it was an on-off sort of thing, I'd see him and stay with him when his boat was in, then he'd be off again for several weeks.

One night a girl I was friendly with, who worked in one of the pubs in the town, she told me there was a Dutch boat had come in. She said a lot of these Dutch sailors were coming to the pub later that night for a drink, and asked me if I'd like to come. I went along there about nine o'clock and there were three or four of the Dutch seamen in the pub, all very merry and drinking. When it got to closing time, two of them asked my friend and me if we'd like to go back to the docks with them and on to their boat. We said Yes, so we all got a taxi and went.

When we got there, how it'd come about I don't know, but none of us had the money with us to pay the taxi driver.

He said he was staying there on the quay until he got it. The Dutch man I was with hardly spoke any English, but he seemed to be saying or I thought he was, that he'd got English money in his cabin and we'd go and get it. There was only a narrow sort of gangplank between the side of the dock and the boat, and he started to pull me across it. My friend and her friend the other Dutchman stayed and waited for us by the taxi. Then about half-way across this plank, the Dutchman who'd had quite a lot to drink and I had too, between us we managed to drop my handbag down by the ship's side into the water. But we got across finally, and we went a little way along the deck of the boat, and then we turned off into a little corridor. A few doors along was his cabin, and as we went along one of the other doors was open with its light on inside. I could see it was the ship's kitchen, the galley they call it I think.

When we got into the man's cabin, he started to take his shirt and trousers off, and he was trying to pull me on to his bunk with him. I know I was drunk, but I wasn't so drunk I was willing to do what he wanted there and then like that. I hadn't forgotten the taxi driver and the other two waiting on the quayside either. I started shouting at him 'Money, money!', meaning for the taxi. He started shouting back at me: that I was a whore and a tart, and he'd give me money afterwards but not before:

I can only say that I've never done anything like it in my whole life, even so much as hit someone. But I turned round and went along to the galley place, and I went back again to the cabin. When I went in he was lying back on his bunk in just his underpants, and his eyes were shut and he was snoring. He was only pretending to be asleep though: when I bent over to look at him, he suddenly opened his eyes and made a grab for me. I brought the knife round from behind my back where I'd been holding it and I stabbed him. I was completely cold; I went on stabbing him, six times altogether, five times in his chest and once in his neck.

He didn't make any noise, just gave a sort of gasp that's all and lay there with his eyes staring. On a shelf by his bunk was his wallet, and I took some money out, two five-pound notes I believe it was. Then I came back on to the deck of the boat, dropped the knife over the side and walked back over the plank to the taxi. I wasn't drunk, what I'd done had made me feel completely sober. There was only the driver there, I don't know where my friend and her chap had gone. I gave him the five-pound notes and asked him to take me to a motel where I'd arranged to meet the Danish man later. When I got there I went to our room and he was already in bed sleeping. I got undressed and climbed in bed with him and I asked him to make love with me but he was fast asleep.

I'm sorry. That's it. I'm so sorry, I'm so sorry.

– I'm sorry about yesterday. Thank you for leaving the cigarettes for me. I haven't talked about it for a long time. Someone once told me I should, talk about it more often and cry. Tears don't count though do they? You can't bring someone back. It's awful isn't it? I don't even know who he was. He probably had a wife and children even, and one day someone had to go and tell her he'd been found murdered on that boat he worked on, lying on his bunk in his under-pants, stabbed to death by an English prostitute in Bristol.

I'm not going to cry about it again today though. I've got to think about things in the future more now haven't I eh? There's my daughter coming next week, that's something I'm getting quite excited about. I didn't think I would you know, it's funny: I've been telling myself I'll be calm and collected about it, not put too much store on it. It won't be a very nice experience for her will it though? All your life you don't know who your mother is or anything about her, then when you do find out she's in prison doing a life sentence for murder. I should think her boyfriend'll be bound to feel a bit peculiar about it too. I hope he won't think afterwards he doesn't want to have any more to do with her. She didn't tell me anything in her letter much about him: all she said was they were getting married in June, she hoped I liked

him, she was sure I would. I hope he's a nice kind person: I
should think she deserves someone like that.

I don't know how much to tell her about my case, my trial
and everything. I suppose the best thing's to wait and see
how much she wants to know. I wonder if she'll be the sort
of person where we can keep in touch now and again,
Christmas and birthday cards and things like that. I was the
sort who didn't want to know anything about my own
mother at all. She had me and she gave me away, that was
how I looked at it; I didn't want to know why or what for,
whether she was having a difficult time or anything. So my
daughter's not like me is she in that?

One thing I have made my mind up to is I'm not going to
ask her a whole lot of questions all at once. If it's her who
asks me the questions, then I'll answer every one as fully
and honestly as I can. I won't make any excuses for myself,
none at all. If she wants to that's for her, not for me. And
her life, I'll leave it for her to tell me what she wants to when
she wants to: I don't have the right to ask her any questions.
The same with whether she wants to keep in touch or not,
she'll have to be the one to decide that. I didn't keep in
touch with her so I'm not the one to say am I? I'd understand easily if she didn't.

One thing that would be very nice if it happened though,
is if she said something that made me feel perhaps one day
she might think of me as a real person to her. If something
like that happened, that'd please me very much. I can't say
what sort of thing it would be: I'm not very clever, I'm not
very good with words. I was trying to write a letter last week
to a friend who's not long gone out. But I couldn't say what
I wanted at all, I didn't seem to know how to put things into
words.

All right. Let me have a think a minute. I'll see if I can
find a way of saying what I'm trying to say about my
daughter, feeling I was a real person in her life. Yes I know
what might be an example: say perhaps when we're talking,
she says a word quite ordinarily and naturally, perhaps
doesn't even notice she's said it. Well what it would be

would be just one nice word: it'd be if she once called me
'Mum'. Just once without even thinking about it. I'm sure
that sounds silly but it's the nearest I can get.

Shall I tell you something I want to know about her, one
thing most of all? You'll probably think it's silly. All my
life, I don't know where I've got it from, but I've always
been fond of music played on a guitar. There's someone
called Segovia is it? I'm not musical, I can't sing or play
anything myself, I don't know a note. But whenever I hear a
guitar playing a nice piece of music, I always get this feeling
I'd really love to be able to do that. There's another one, I
think his name's John Williams. Sometimes I hear him on
the radio and it's lovely, he's the best one there is. Wouldn't
it be funny if my daughter had got that in her as well? I
wonder if she has? You make up a picture of a person in
your mind don't you? You shouldn't though because you
only disappoint yourself if they're not like that. She sent me
a little photo of herself: one of those you get from an
automatic machine, you draw a curtain and put money in
and it takes it of you. I couldn't tell much about her from it,
she said it wasn't a very good one. And she's got no idea
what I look like at all. Perhaps she'll think I've got fangs,
and horns coming out of my head eh?

Oh dear that's quite enough now about me and my
daughter isn't it? I keep telling myself to stop thinking
about it but you can't help it. Yesterday at tea-time
everyone was jolly and laughing, and I looked at one girl
who'd be about the same age as Stella; I thought the best
thing to do would be write and say I'd thought it over,
perhaps it'd be better if she didn't come after all. I don't
know what made me think it. The girl was swearing and
using a lot of four-letter words and things. I mean I've done
it myself, it's easy to get like that in these places. But I
thought I wouldn't like it if Stella did it; that isn't very
sensible of me is it?

Oh there's the tea bell, is it that time already? I'm sorry I
don't seem to have talked much today about anything, only
about my daughter coming. There were things I was going

to say about being in prison but I haven't seemed to have said much about that. Next time though then eh?

– No I didn't, it was just a panic. I left it like it was. I didn't put her off so they're coming on Sunday, the day after tomorrow. I had a letter from her this morning confirming it, saying they're looking forward to it. They're going to drive all the way up from London in his car, it's a long way for them to come isn't it? I wonder what sort of a car it is, perhaps he's got a very good job? He's Indian she said, they work hard don't they? Still no more about my daughter this time, I'm not going to talk about it or even think about it. Just keep my fingers crossed for Sunday eh?

Altogether prison's changed my life every way. You'll think it's strange to hear someone say this, but in some ways it's been the best period in my life, specially since I came here. First of all I was in Holloway, then I went to the women's wing at Durham, then to the semi-open prison at Styal for three years, then finally three years ago I came here. It's completely open, but I've not done anything stupid like absconding like when I was a kid at approved school. I'm grateful for what's been done for me, I've behaved myself all the way through, and it's paid off because now I know the date when I'm going out, where I'm going to go and to some extent what my future's going to be.

All the same it's a terrible thing to say though isn't it, it was only at the expense of someone else's life that I finally got my own sorted out? He died, I killed him, and that's something I've got to live with, that I murdered a man. The way I was going, I suppose I could easily have ended up being the one who was killed. You hear more of it that way round don't you, women going with men they don't know and being murdered?

There are two main things prison's done for me. The first one is that if what happened hadn't happened, I'm fairly sure I would have ended up being an alcoholic, perhaps gone even further down from there. Drugs, prostitution, and what else after that I don't know. In prison if you've got problems there's always people you can go and talk about them with; I don't know if it's the same in men's prisons, I expect there's too many of them for them to get individual attention. But in women's prisons, someone's always got time for you, to sit and listen to you and try and help you sort things out. They want to help you: they do try to, and I'd say they mostly do a good job. I think you have to be a certain age before you can benefit though. There's a lot of these young girls, they want to be tough: and they are tough, very very tough some of them. I think it's sad, they don't know what they're doing to themselves. But whatever it is, it's not good. I suppose you've got to remember they've had rough lives themselves otherwise they wouldn't be here. One or two of them, they talk to me sometimes because I'm an older woman: a bit motherly perhaps, and they think I'm wiser than they are. I'm not, in a lot of ways I'm just as stupid as they are. I wish I could help some of them more, some are decent girls at heart. I don't have training for that sort of thing: you do need training, and to get it you need to be clever and intelligent, which I'm not.

The other thing which prison has done for me, well this is a very personal thing. It's woken me up would be one way of putting it: woken me up to what sort of person I am, which is something I'd never realized in my whole life until up to now. I used to think there was something wrong with me but I'd no idea what. It's only now, very late on in life I've found out what it was. Perhaps it's too early to say yet, but I've had a window opened, it might even be a door.

It began when I was at Styal. You do get a certain amount of freedom there: you live in groups in different buildings, they call them houses. In the evenings you go in communal association rooms and watch the telly or play cards, or put records on the record player. Usually it was all too lively and noisy for me, so I always went in one of the side rooms and joined in a card game, or sat around with everyone else chatting. I wasn't a person who made friends easily, I think

I had a reputation for being stand-offish, not someone who either wanted to get to know people or let herself get to be known.

It was always more or less the same group of us in the room: six or seven, always the same ones on the whole. I was the oldest one there by quite a lot. One evening one of the officers put her head round the door at nine o'clock or whatever it was, to tell us it was bedtime like usual, then when she went off we started to clear the cards and tables as normal. I was putting the cards away in a cupboard; when I turned round there was one of the girls in the group who'd come and was standing behind me. She was very young, about twenty, she was a coloured girl and her name was Barbara. She didn't draw any attention to herself, I think the others were clearing away and weren't noticing. She put her arms round me and kissed me full on the mouth, on my lips; she whispered 'Good night Carol love,' then she turned round and walked out.

The feeling I had just completely knocked me out. It was so unexpected, no woman had ever done something like that to me, I just stood there with my head in a complete whirl. And what I found so overwhelming about it was I didn't recoil or think she shouldn't have done it: I found it tremendously exciting and stirring, I was thrilled.

The next night we were all in the room again, the same group of us playing cards exactly the same way. Barbara was completely casual, chatting and laughing with everyone like she always did. I sat there feeling like a jelly, my stomach was churning over, I couldn't take my eyes off her. After a while I had to put my cards down, I couldn't go on playing; I said I wasn't feeling well, I was going to bed. I got up and went out, and I suppose I was hoping she'd follow me but she didn't. I don't think she even looked up.

I felt like what had happened must have been a dream, I must have imagined it. But only a day or two later I found out it wasn't, it was for real. So we became lovers, we had a proper love affair. I knew it could only be short because Barbara'd only got a few more weeks before her sentence finished and she was going out. When she did, I didn't let myself get broken-hearted about it: it had been mainly just a physical love affair, and I'd enjoyed it. I've never seen her or heard from her since, but I don't mind: I shall always be very very grateful to her for doing what she did, which was wake me up sexually.

It was something I'd never imagined could happen, or that it could even exist between women. The idea of two women making love to each other I'd always thought was a very strange one. I don't think so now, it's not strange at all; what I do know now is I could never ever think about doing it again with a man. I always found at least with those I went with, they didn't believe in foreplay to turn you on a bit: all they wanted was their own climax, then as soon as they'd had that, that was the end of it. Whereas with a woman, they get pleasure out of giving it her, as well as enjoying it themselves. I can get very excited and be completely unin-hibited in sex now; I'm not like that in any other way at all, normally I'm a person who's very very shy like I said. I don't know if men understand this, I think a lot of them think it's disgusting. But it doesn't matter to me now though if they do or they don't. I know what I want out of sex, and of life too, and I'm going to stay like I am for good.

There is a particular reason for saying it, yes. What I've been telling you, I hope I've not given the idea that now I've found out what I am, I'm a woman madly going round looking for sex. I'm not. I've had two brief love affairs that's all. In these places you don't get much opportunity for anything else, but I don't just mean because there aren't men around or like it was with Barbara, there's no chance for something long term.

You see in that respect, I've been a very lucky person: because what I've had and still have is a relationship that's lasted for a long time. It's been over a year and it's still going on. There's another prisoner who came in at the beginning of last summer, and we're in love with each other. It's very deep and very real, and we both feel the same about it. We're both sure it's much more than just a prison love affair, and it really will last. You can't say for life, you never can with things like that; anyway it's unlucky to say it, it's tempting fate. But we talk about it over and over. I think we've faced what it means, and decided what we have, that when we're both out we're going to live together. It's not just a sex thing: that's part of it, an important part; but we talk together as well, we share things, we don't have any secrets from each other, we love each other and what's more important we like each other too.

She went out two months ago. She's already found a council house for us, and we exchange letters every week. She sent me flowers for my birthday last month, and we're both feeling calm and sensible about it. There are difficulties about how much you can say in letters between you when one's still in prison; there might be a problem about her getting permission to come and see me too, on a visit, they're not keen on ex-prisoners doing that. Still, we're working on it, we're both happy about it, and we're keeping our fingers crossed it comes out right in the end.

'It was very kind of you to send me the tape recording of John Williams playing that lovely music. One of the girls has got a tape player, she lends it to me so I can have a listen to it. It's lovely. Thank you very much. My visit with my daughter all went off OK, and her fiancey (if that's how you spell it) seemed a nice young man and both of them very fond of each other. She said they'd like to keep in touch with me, she's given me her address where they'll be living when they get married. It will be in London so perhaps I can go there and see them one day. Keep your fingers crossed for me. Thank you again for sending me the tape. With love from Carol. XX'

FOUR

A perfectly ordinary normal person

PAUL ARROWSMITH

– He's such a perfectly ordinary normal person, his probation officer said, you couldn't possibly imagine meeting him and talking to him there's anything different about him to anyone else at all. He's a murderer only been out of prison on licence less than a year so far? If you told that to someone sitting next to him on a bus they wouldn't believe you, they'd laugh and say you were pulling their leg.

Tall, well built, pale complexioned with short fair hair and hazel eyes, he wore a faded blue striped T-shirt, old trainers and patched jeans. He sat in the office in a swivel chair, turning it slowly from one side to the other as he talked, his arms up in the air and his hands clasped behind his head.

– I woke up I suppose about seven o'clock last Saturday morning in this little country pub we stay at, Jennifer was still sound asleep. I thought I wouldn't wake her up because of the long drive up she'd had to do the night before. I got dressed and went downstairs and no one else was up, there wasn't a soul to be seen anywhere in the entrance hall or the bar. So I unlocked the front door and let myself out, and outside everything was fresh and clear in beautiful brilliant sunshine. I walked down the road till I came to a little bridge and crossed it, then followed the path along by the side of the river. Through a wood with the birds singing, across a meadow with sheep in it, up a hill and down the other side. And then I came out on the shore at the end of I think it's Derwentwater: a fantastic sight, I've never seen anything like it in my life. The sky was blue, there wasn't a cloud in it anywhere, you could almost taste the air. It was so crisp and clean you felt you could almost drink it. All round the side of the lake the mountains were different shades of greens and browns and greys, and they were all reflected in the water that was flat and still and glittering in the sunlight. One of the most beautiful pieces of scenery I've ever seen, just like a picture book, it was absolutely fantastic.

But the only thing I felt was sick, and I started to tremble and sweat. Because I suddenly thought Jesus Christ, what am I going to say on Tuesday? And how can I say it and not sound as though I'm totally cold-blooded and heartless, how can I talk in a calm or detached way of any sort without seeming not to have got any human feelings at all?

It stayed with me all weekend. The weather was absolutely perfect both Saturday and Sunday and we did a lot of driving around. Jennifer kept stopping the car in different places so we could get out and have walks. Now and again she commented on how beautiful it was, how it'd never looked so marvellous ever before. I was terrible company, I hardly said a word the whole two days. She knows I get bad periods of depression and understands, so as usual she didn't ask for explanations or question me about it or ask why. But all I could think of was how closer today kept coming. I was thinking over and over to myself Jesus Christ, however'll I find the words?

Anyway anyway anyway: now we're here, now it's now. I wanted to say that first though, to get it off my chest. So right yes OK let's begin.

Start where I like? All right, I'm thirty-five, about six foot tall, getting a bit fat round the middle, I've got fair hair and greeny brown eyes, I'm wearing an old T-shirt and old jeans, and a pair of not very presentable running shoes. I'm a clerk in an office and today I've got a day off. When I'm at work I wear a collar and tie and suit, which I hate because I'm not used to clothes like that, and as soon as I can when I get home I change into more comfortable old things like this. I've been outside prison two years now; or I've been out five months, depending on what's called being inside. Two years ago I was still in prison but I was put on a working-out hostel for the remainder of my time before my release date. I went to work every day from the hostel and then back to it at night; then five months ago I was let out completely and moved off the hostel into digs of my own.

Now I'm stuck. I don't know that all that prison and hostel stuff's of any great interest really, so I'll try something else. Work. Where I work, I'm a clerk in an office of a small engineering firm: it's not very well paid but it's easy work, pushing bits of paper around, invoices, doing some filing and stuff like that. The job was got for me in the first place by the prison people when I was first moved to the hostel. There are six people in the office: the manager who's a man of about fifty who's in charge of it all, four married women who are part-time clerks, and myself. Which of the people I work with knows where I come from and what my background is, that I'm a life-sentence prisoner et cetera et cetera, I've no idea. Some days I think none of them do, everyone's jolly and friendly and perfectly natural; other days there seems to be an atmosphere in the office, which may have something to do with me or it might not. That's one of the after-effects of being a lifer: when the slightest little thing goes wrong or someone's a bit hostile to you – at work, a bus conductor, someone in a shop – your first thought's always it's due to you, they can see the mark of Cain on your forehead. Or is it Abel? No I think I got it right first time, it's Cain.

Jesus Christ this is a ramble. My probation officer said to me once I was loquacious but not garrulous. I report to him here every week. Apart from my life sentence, I don't have a previous criminal record. No, to be strictly correct I should say I do have one but it's hardly very serious, only a juvenile one. Or perhaps to be even more strictly correct I should say it's only me that says it isn't a very serious one: someone else might have a different view on it. It was nineteen years ago when I was sixteen. Like a lot of youngsters that age I was a bit of a rowdy when I got with a gang of my mates. We were all into motor bikes, and I lived dreamed slept ate thought nothing but motor bikes. Finally I got done for riding one

without L plates, then a week later for stealing one, riding it
without a licence or insurance or anything else, and ended
up doing three months in a juvenile detention centre followed with three years on probation. The probation officer
was good and he talked some sense into me: he got me to
take lessons and pass my driving test with a van, then he got
me on a training course to qualify as a television set instal-
ler, and after that he found me a job with one of the TV
rental companies. I was a juvenile delinquent who saw the
error of his ways, was given a chance, took it and made
good. End of juvenile delinquency.

Jesus I'm not making a very good job of this. Anyway:
the point of what I'm trying to say is that in the one instance
apart, which in some respects you could call an ordinary
run-of-the-mill bit of juvenile offending, there's nothing
else in my history that could be taken as a pointer to what
was to come. I read a book once when I was in prison – in
prison you get a lot of time for reading – about people who
did murders, and it said in nearly every case there was a sort
of inevitability in their earlier lives, leading up to what they
were going to do. You could see it coming. I don't think
that was true in my case: the violence wasn't foreshadowed
you might say, not in any way at all. That was why it came
as a shock and why it still remains a shock, I mean to me.
Now thirteen years later when I look back on it, I still can't
grasp it. It was like something that happened to someone
else, and I find myself saying 'How could he possibly do it?'
Only then I realize that that 'he' I'm referring to is me. It
doesn't seem like me, all the time it seems like 'he' or 'him'.
Jesus Christ I find this difficult, I'm not making any sense at
all am I? I'll sit and think for a minute.

Anyway anyway, right well try again. I'll try and come at
it from a different direction. Childhood: the child is father
to the man et cetera et cetera. Childhood, what shall I say
about my childhood: I was born in Swindon, I grew up and
went to school there?

No, that's no good. Come on Paul, get it over: it might
not be as bad as you think and you never know, afterwards

it might be a bit better. Big breath. So OK we're two blokes sitting in a pub somewhere, having a quiet drink together and a chat. We haven't known each other long. I ask you what you do, you tell me a bit about yourself; then you ask me what I do, you say tell you a bit about myself. So I say Right. Very casual, matter-of-fact, just the same way as you told me about you. And what do I say? This.

Thirteen years ago when I was twenty-three, I battered a man to death with a car starting-handle. He wasn't someone I knew, it wasn't during a quarrel or a fight; I'd never even spoken to him before, and in fact he was asleep at the time in his room, a furnished bed-sitter on the opposite side of the first-floor landing to the one I had, in a lodging house in Northampton. I didn't know what his name was then and I still don't know it now, and I don't know how old he was except I believe he was someone of about my own age.

And I did it because under my bed in my room I kept an old trunk I took around with me, with all my worldly possessions in it. There were some clothes, a few bits and pieces of personal possessions, shoes, some spanners, and one or two motor car tools: the ordinary collection of things a lot of working men have. I'd been working all week on a scaffolding job for a big building and road-making company in a town nearby, and Friday night I'd been out for a few drinks on my own like I usually did. Maybe I had a few too many. That's not an excuse though: if I did, it wouldn't have been the first time, and I remember what I did, I don't claim not to. It would have been ten o'clock when I got back to the lodgings, or perhaps a bit later. I don't remember the reason but I wanted something out of the box and I pulled it out from under the bed. I think I wanted to look at a new adjustable wrench I'd bought: and it wasn't there. Immediately and straight away, without so much as a second thought about it I was certain I knew who'd taken it: it was the bastard from over the other side of the landing. As far as I knew he'd never been in my room ever before, and I'd never shown him the

Life After Life

wrench or told him about it. But that didn't come into my mind: I just knew instantly it was him that'd taken it.

I took a big car starting-handle out of the box, walked across the landing and went to his door; it wasn't locked, so I pushed it open, switched on his light, and went in. He was lying in bed with his back to me, fast asleep. I didn't say anything, didn't wake him up and accuse him of thieving my gear or anything like that; I just hit him over the head with the car handle, and went on hitting him and hitting him. I don't know how many times I hit him altogether, but it was a lot: more than twelve I think they said in court.

Then I went along the landing to the bathroom, and I was violently sick. That immediately sobered me up completely. I had blood all over my hands and arms and I washed it off as well as I could, then I went back to my room and changed my clothes. After that I just flopped into an armchair and I went straight off to sleep. I kept waking up and falling back asleep again, and some time in the early hours next morning I went back across the landing to his room again to make sure I hadn't dreamed it all. I hadn't. He was dead, his head was smashed in, there was blood all over everywhere, his head and face and bedclothes and spattered on the wall. I pulled out one or two drawers from the wardrobe and threw things around on the floor, and opened a suitcase and scattered its contents about, to make it look like there'd been a robbery I suppose.

After that I'm not sure what I did for most of the rest of the morning. Mainly walked about in the town in a daze I think. I remember I saw a poster somewhere, advertising a fête there was going to be that afternoon in the gardens of a stately home. I had a few lunch-time beers in a pub, wandered around the town for a while again; then I went out to this country house place where the fête was. There were all the things they always have: crowds of people, stalls, roundabouts, sideshows, pony rides, a miniature steam train, and I think there was a hot air balloon. The sun was shining, everyone enjoying themselves, parents buying their kids ice-creams, all laughing and chatting. I remember one of the main attractions was a group dressed up in furry animal costumes, wearing funny faces and hats and dancing around. I think they were called 'The Wombles of Wimbledon'. I was standing in the middle of a whole group of kids watching them. And I suddenly realized my face was all wet, tears were pouring down my cheeks and wouldn't stop.

I knew I couldn't stay there any longer. I left the fête and went back to the town to the lodging house, and went back upstairs to my room. I thought I'd check, so I went across the landing: I just looked at the bloke's room, and everything was exactly the same as I'd left it. He was still lying covered in blood in the bed, the drawers were pulled out and the things in them scattered around. In the hall downstairs there was a public phone so I went down to it and rang up the police. I said I'd just come in and it looked as though there'd been a robbery and a fight in the room opposite mine, and I thought someone had been badly hurt. The police told me not to touch anything, they told me to go back in my room and wait for them.

They came and took me down to the police station and they sat me down in a room and gave me a cup of tea, and then they asked me a few questions. Two plain-clothes policemen came in, and in an ordinary tone of voice one of them said 'You did it, did you son?' I nodded; I said 'Yes that's right I did.'

So. Anyway anyway. That's about the best I can do.

— I thought I might feel better for having got it all over in one go yesterday, but I don't in the sense that it in any way makes me feel less bad about it. But well anyway now you know the worst part, so the rest can't help but be not quite so bad. Least I'm not dreading coming round to it, but that's about as much as I can say. To tell someone you've been a complete animal, behaved like a homicidal maniac, even if it was a long time earlier in your life, it still doesn't alter the fact that for all the rest of your life you go on

thinking about it. I've long ago given up hope I'd ever find
the answer to the question why I did it. Now what's much
more worrying to me is a different question I go on asking
myself, which is would I ever do it again? And the only
honest answer to that one is I don't know; but what I do
know is it's a pretty frightening thought to live with. And I
should get out of the habit of talking like that about it too,
and be honest. I should say it's not a frightening thought:
it's a fucking terrifying one.

When I got back to my digs last night and was thinking it
over, I remember I think I said saying I'd been drinking and
had had a few too many, but wasn't offering that as an
excuse. Only saying it like that, behind it there was a
suggestion it's not an excuse but OK it is a reason. But it
isn't: it's nothing like a reason, not at all. Lots of people,
thousands of them, perhaps even tens of thousands of them,
get drunk on a Friday night or at a weekend. But not one in
ten thousand, not one in a hundred thousand goes back to
where they're living and batters a complete stranger to
death. Possibly in similar circumstances they might just
conceivably go over to his room and wake him up and say
'Why've you taken my adjustable wrench, you thieving
bastard?' They might, just. But that's still a long way short
of what I did. It is, it's frightening. No there you are you
see, I've done it again. Come on Paul. Right then: it's not
frightening, it's fucking terrifying.

Anyway anyway. One more thing first though, something
else that came into my mind last night. I started wondering
how often something like that happens, well one aspect of it
at least. I'd been saying how I didn't know the man I killed,
how I thought he was probably living the sort of rootless
vagrant life that I was. I have a feeling he might have come
over from Ireland; but that's only a vague idea and I don't
know where I got it from. I went on thinking about it last
night, and I thought it could just as easily have been the
other way round. You know, me the unknown man instead,
killed by another unknown man. When I was tried there
were no newspaper headlines, it was an absolutely

unnoticed event. I pleaded guilty and it was all over in two minutes at the most. No one in court except legal people and police, no witnesses, no doctors' reports read out. I'd been examined once when I was on remand by a psychiatrist: he said he couldn't detect any sign of insanity or abnormality, I was perfectly normal mentally et cetera et cetera, and knew all the time exactly what I was doing. And that was all there was to it, the whole thing was a complete non-event. It kept me awake quite a while last night, thinking about that: how something so drastic as one human being killing another, how it could pass virtually unnoticed and for ever afterwards be completely forgotten as though nobody anywhere had even so much as noticed it. I thought about it, and I think it's weird, quite weird.

But you know even now while I talk about it, nobody knowing him: I suppose it wasn't all that much more strange than my own situation either, come to think about it. After I'd come out of the detention centre I left home and took up with a girl, and then she and I moved around the country a lot. I don't know if her parents knew where she was, but mine didn't know where I was, for the simple reason I never bothered to let them know or tried to keep in touch. One day, I can't even remember how it came about now, but I heard from someone I met who I knew vaguely that my mother had died. I went back home on a visit, but that wasn't a good idea. As a child when I was younger I knew she and my father hadn't got on together all that well. But that didn't stop my father from telling me when I went home that I'd not behaved properly towards her: they hadn't heard from me for over a year and she'd missed me and been lonely. He sounded as though he was trying to make me feel responsible in some way for her dying. I expect I sound callous talking like this. If I am though it's partly to do with the fact as you'll have gathered, we'd never been a close or affectionate family. It can't have been all that long afterwards I heard my father had died too. Then finally the girl and I, we broke up as well, and she went off with another bloke. I talk about these things as though they were news items I read about in the paper don't I? In many ways you know that's exactly how they seemed at the time, as though they were things that happened to other people and weren't really much concern of mine.

Have I ever had a sustained relationship? Ever in my life you mean? Jesus Christ that's a hard question to try and answer. I'll have to think about it. I'm not sure in what respect we're talking about sustained, in length or sustained in depth? Either yes; well of course. Christ. I can't give a quick answer: I want to give it a bit of thought. You see in a funny way it's got something to do with prison, which I haven't said much about yet. In fact it's got more than something to do with prison, it's got everything to do with prison. I'll have to lead into the subject gradually though, one thing's connected with another. There's someone else concerned, and I ought to talk to them about it first.

– When I went into prison at the start of my sentence, I had the feeling very strongly inside me that I was trying to explain that what had happened, hadn't really happened to me. It had happened to somebody else and really had nothing much to do with me at all. That might sound as though I'm saying I was schizophrenic; except that I don't know what schizophrenia is. Nobody's ever said to me that I was, and I'm not trying to offer a diagnosis.

It sounds a contradiction in terms to say the thing I was most conscious of was that I wasn't conscious of being anybody. I'd had several months in prison in custody waiting to be tried; nobody'd written or been to see me, so far as I could tell nobody knew me or wanted to know me. To all events and purposes it seemed I might just as well have not existed as far as the outside world was concerned. I was in prison, and in prison I was a name and a number, and that was all there was to me. When the Judge said he was sentencing me to life imprisonment, it didn't seem to have any meaning. I could almost say it didn't even seem to have any reference to me as a person. I expected a life sentence, I knew I was going to get a life sentence; but I didn't think of it in terms of a certain limited number of years. I didn't have any reason to. To me life meant life, full stop. If I was going to die say when I was forty that was how long my sentence would be; if I died at forty-five, then the sentence would be until I was forty-five. I couldn't see it any other way, and I couldn't see there was any other way to see it.

I don't know how I can put it properly. I think the nearest I can get to it is to say it was like someone taking you to a different country and when you got there telling you you were never going anywhere else, you were going to live there for ever. The other country I'd been taken to was prison, and I was going to be a citizen of prison, I was going to learn its language and adopt its customs, live in it totally and never again know anything different. I wasn't bitter and I didn't have any sense of loss of a former existence, I was there in total acceptance and anyway it wasn't really happening to me in the first place.

I didn't know it at the time, but I've since found out that as a matter of fact actually that's not an uncommon experience for a lot of men at the start of a long sentence. Apparently they feel like that, or anyway most of them do, for their first four or five years. I read it was described somewhere as 'the acceptance period'; it's the time a man has to spend before it starts to occur to him this is only the beginning of the sentence and he won't go on necessarily feeling like it for ever. It's got something to do with human nature they say: after a time things begin to stir in a man's mind. Hope springs eternal et cetera, something of that sort.

It was true in my case, it was exactly like that. The first years, four or perhaps five, I was in a kind of shell. I never made any approaches towards talking to anyone at all, whether they were the authorities or the other prisoners or anyone. Long-sentence prisoners generally don't; someone doing say two or three years, he's just a man in off the street for a few days. I just existed that's all: slept, got up, ate meals, did whatever the work was I was put on – sweeping, cleaning, laundry, maintenance, prison gardens – then went back to eat another meal again and go to bed. There was what they call 'association', a couple of hours in the early evening after tea when you're out of your cell and can watch the telly or sit around and talk, play table tennis, weight-lifting in the gym, anything you feel like. For me, all I ever did was watch TV; I don't think in the whole of three or perhaps four years I spoke to anyone, or at least not in any kind of social sense.

What I mean by that is that that was only a half of my existence. There was another half of me as well: a com-pletely different one, and also very very different to the quiet retiring-into-a-shell one I've been talking about. The other half was the big arguer and trouble-maker, who was constantly rowing and shouting and throwing his weight about, both with the other prisoners and even more with the authorities and staff. I didn't fight physically because I'm not a fighter: but any quarrel that blew up, any complaint, any protest of any sort about anything and everything it didn't matter what, I was immediately right in there mixing it. They took privileges away from me, they fined me, they threatened me with losing parole, they put me in solitary confinement, everything they could think of. None of it made any difference at all: it didn't stop me for one minute from going around and finding some trouble I could get myself involved in. An easy thing to say about it was that I was trying to find an identity for myself, or if I couldn't find one then I'd make one as a well known trouble-maker.

Yet all the time, at the same time I was still doing this thing of standing outside and watching it happen, and feeling it'd got nothing whatsoever to do with me. I suppose that was how I could keep it up for as long as I did, if you like by not feeling the person they were punishing was me. It went on and on for over four years; how much longer still it would have continued after that if something else hadn't happened, God only knows. I was moved to this prison, that prison, the other prison, almost every single one there is.

Gartree, Bristol, Hull, Preston, Blundeston, Lewes, et cetera et cetera – the whole lot. And wherever I went, I went on with the arguing, the breaking the rules, the bloody-mindedness, every chance I got. Now and again an Assistant Governor would take it into his head that he might be the one person in the world who could get through to me and talk some sense into me: several tried but none of them got anywhere, not one single bloody one.

Anyway anyway I could go on about prison as much or more than most. But what happened was that one day in one of the prisons I was at, I'm not even sure which one it was now, anyway they asked me would I like to see a psychologist. This wasn't out of any desire to help me, it was only because some kind of statistical study was being done and they wanted to make the numbers up. A hundred men six foot tall, eighty-two of them right-handed, all born between June ten and July twenty-first, something of that sort. I wasn't doing anything else at the time, it wasn't going to interfere with my holiday arrangements for a trip to Switzerland so I thought OK why not? A few days later or perhaps a week, they trundled me along to the psychologist's office along with a couple of other blokes, and we all sat at desks and did one of these what do you call them, tick tests. 'If you saw a cat run over by a steamroller what would your reaction be: burst into tears, burst out laughing, get angry with the steamroller driver, call it an act of God, or shrug your shoulders and walk away? Tick which one is closest to what you think your reaction would be. Question Two: 'If you saw a little old lady run over by a steamroller et cetera.' You get lots of that sort of thing in prison, after a while you do them with your eyes shut, or according to what you think makes a nice looking pattern. Then they gather them all up, put them into a computer, and it comes out the other end that the best colour to repaint the walls in the workshop would be bright green.

I didn't think any more about it at the time. About another week after that, then I got asked to go and see the psychologist again. Naturally I told them to eff off saying

I'd already done it, and they should go and get some other mug for it. But they said no, this was a different section of it: the three of us who'd been before were wanted back for the next part. So off we all went again, and this time we sat round in a little group in the psychologist's office, and she asked us a list of questions in turn and wrote down our individual answers.

I thought well anyway, it passes the time: it was boring but it made a change. That was about the total extent I thought about it, I can't say it made any more impression on me than that. And then when I was asked a third time to go again, this time on my own to answer even more questions, I really made up mind that enough was enough and I wasn't going to co-operate any more.

I still don't know what made me change my mind. I can only say pure chance, when the time came it was no more than how I happened to feel on the spur of the moment. I won't go; I'm definitely not going; Oh all right I might as well, I've nothing else to do. The interview I had on my own, there was nothing memorable about it: just more questions, fill in this diagram, which of these five pictures is the odd one out et cetera, no more than that. At the end she told me the experiment or whatever it was she was doing was over, she'd got all the material she needed, and thanked me for taking part. Then just as I was going out of her office door, she said very casually if I wanted to any time, I could always drop in for a chat. It was merely a politeness thing: see you again sometime, let me know if I can ever do a good turn for you in return.

About two weeks later I was sitting around doing nothing after my dinner, and for some reason I thought I know what I'll do, I'll do what she said and drop in on her for a chat. So I went to her office, but she was busy seeing someone else. I went back again a day or two afterwards instead, and we had our chat: it was very superficial, about something and nothing, it didn't last more than ten minutes at the outside if that. The next week I went to see her again, I dropped in for another chat; and then again the week after that.

There's nothing uncommon about men in prison falling in love with some female or other they come across there: in fact it's so common I'd say almost every one in two does it. The only alternative's to fall for other men, be temporarily gay, what they call 'prison bent'. I've known men having a visit look across the visiting room at some other bloke's sister who's talking to him, and without ever having met her fall madly in love with her, offering the bloke a fortune in tobacco to give him her name and address.

It wasn't exactly like that with Jennifer: in fact for a long time she was just someone I went and talked to now and again for a brief chat, I told myself it was just something to pass the time. We never talked about anything personal: she didn't ask me about my background and I didn't ask her about hers. In fact the only thing personal I knew about her at all was she was married, because she had a wedding ring on her finger.

Very early on we were both aware of what'd happened and that we'd fallen in love with each other. But there seemed to be no shyness in saying it and no shyness in talking about it, and that's always been one of the features of our relationship ever since. We've both always talked openly with each other about things. We regarded ourselves as lovers, which we were, and it went on in that way to begin with for almost a year. I suppose there are more hopeless situations to be in if you're in love with someone than that, but I can't think of one. Doing a life sentence and being in love with a woman who only comes in the prison two days a week and is married to someone else outside is not exactly an everyday situation. We weren't lovers in a physical sense because that wasn't possible under the circumstances, but in every other way we were. We kept going because we knew one day the circumstances would change and we'd be able to be together properly. That stopped it being a sad or unhappy thing: it was the best there could be under the circumstances and we both accepted it and tried to be content to wait. Conversation was very restricted naturally, even touching each other wasn't on; yet somehow none of that seemed to matter enough to change things.

Then I got moved on to another prison in the north. My first reaction was that would be the end of it. But the way it turned out, not only didn't it mean that, in fact it made things in a lot of ways easier, because at least then we could write to each other. I'd known at some stage she was separated from her husband, and she changed her name back to her maiden one so I could write to her at her flat in north London. Visits were out though: it was too risky for her to come and see me, in case one of the prison staff who'd been at a place she'd been before recognized her. In the letters we could express our feelings to each other a lot more freely, but we were careful not to mention how we'd first met.

It was good; it was a good period because it opened something up inside me – feelings, affection for someone, love, receiving love and affection back. It wouldn't be right to say it changed me completely, because those things must have been there all the time inside me. I do say though Jennifer saw them, she was aware they were there, and she helped to bring them out. She helped to uncover the softer part of me. Being in prison, half of me was hard and a trouble-maker; the other half fell in love. Both happened at the same time: they were contradictory things but both of them were inside the same person.

So that's the answer to the question on Friday about a sustained relationship. It has been one with Jennifer and it still is, and she said talk about it because she thought it was too. A few minutes ago I used the phrase 'falling in love', and to a lot of people that might suggest infatuation or something like it, rather than real love, particularly under prison circumstances. If it had been only that though, I think it would have been obvious when I was eventually moved on to an open prison and given a release date for a year after that. From then on one of the things I could do was have home leave for weekends so long as I had someone to go and stay with, which I did with Jennifer.

She and her husband had divorced by then; she'd resigned from the prison service and changed to a job with a local authority, in the Midlands. She had a flat and that's where I went for my leaves, staying with her. We didn't talk about it beforehand, but we were both aware of the fact it was going to be a crucial test: we'd had the fantasy, the love affair, and now we were going to have the reality of two human beings actually being in close contact with each other in every way. We'd always been honest with each other since the idea of being able to be together first became a possibility: we said all we could do was try it, and if it didn't work we'd face it. We felt it was a problem we'd deal with if and when it actually happened, not one we could solve in advance by talking about it.

But in fact there wasn't a problem and everything was very simple. Everything was perfectly normal and natural, and there's been no difficulty about it ever. They say that, don't they: it often happens you think there's going to be a problem and then when the time comes it doesn't exist? That's how it was for us, and when I came out of the hostel and moved in to live in the flat permanently, it was already like we'd been together for years. I suppose another thing might one day be a problem too, but so far it's not come up; and again it might do or it might not, how can you tell? Some people would say we're bound to break up, because our age difference is far too great: I'm thirty-five and she's fifty-seven and it's a lot. But all we can do is wait and see.

FIVE

The life and times of an inadequate psychopath

ARTHUR DODDS

He would be willing to co-operate because it might be in the interests of science, he said. In the evenings after everyone else had gone home he sat hunched up in a chair in a corner of the deserted probation office, small and undernourished, talking in a low monotone that sometimes he almost let fade away, as though he was trying to listen himself to what he was saying. He wore a buttoned-up jacket of a double-breasted brown suit, and old black pinstripe trousers; his shirt collar was frayed and his tightly knotted black tie was marked with food stains. A thick moustache and sparse brown hair, motionless hands clasped in his lap. From time to time he gave a small detached laugh. He was forty-one.

– We can't talk at the place I'm living at because it's a hostel and there's nowhere there that's private. It's like a medium-sized detached house in a road not far from Wormwood Scrubs prison, and it's for ex-offenders only.

I've been living there now for fourteen months. It's not too bad, there's twelve men altogether and a warden and his wife, and everyone lives like a family. You have your meals round one big table in the dining-room, then there's a sitting-room where you can sit and read or watch television, and an old-fashioned big kitchen at the back. You take it in turns to do things in the house on a rota system: it's all written up on a sheet of paper pinned on the back of the kitchen door. One week you'll be preparing vegetables and cooking, another week it's your turn for washing up, week three you do cleaning, and it goes on like that.

Every Friday night at half past seven there's what's called a house meeting. Everyone has to attend it, it's compulsory: everyone sits round the dining-room table and any problems

that there've been in the house during the week are cleared
up. Say if two of the residents have had an argument, or one
person's doing something that's annoying someone else.
This is brought up and there's a general discussion, including the warden and his wife, and things get sorted out by
general agreement. The emphasis is on living together as
you would do in a family, and learning how to get on with
other people, something most of the people who go there
haven't had experience of for years because they've been
inside. The bedrooms are shared, two men to a room or
three in some of the bigger ones. You divide the cupboards
and chests of drawers and wardrobes between you, you
make your own bed and keep your part of the room tidy,
and in that way you get experience of sharing your living
space.

There isn't any general rule about it, but on the whole
you don't talk about your crimes. You don't know what
most people there've done and they don't know what you've
done. That's fairly usual in hostels for ex-prisoners I think:
people are trying to put their pasts behind them and build
up a new life for themselves, they're not interested in other
people. As far as I know the warden and his wife are the
only people there who know I've not come out of prison and
that I've come out from Broadmoor. I've not told any of the
other residents and I prefer it that they don't know.

Apart from having to attend the house meeting on a
Friday night, there aren't many other rules and regulations.
One is that you're supposed to have to have a job. If you
haven't you've got to be out looking for one, you're not
allowed to sit round the house all day doing nothing.
Another is you have to be in by eleven o'clock at night, and
you're not allowed to come back the worse for drink. If you
do, you'll get a warning; you might get two warnings
altogether if you're lucky, but the next time after that you're
thrown out. That very rarely happens though, because most
of the men there have been homeless and they're glad to
have somewhere decent to live.

The food isn't bad, it's basic, usually meat and potatoes,

sausages, two veg and pudding. I don't have a big appetite myself, but sometimes at a house meeting you'll get the person who complains about monotonous food. The usual answer to this is they're told to do it better when it's their turn for cooking. The warden is a young chap a bit younger than I am, his name's Malcolm; he's easygoing but tough when he has to be. His wife's called Ann or Annie and she's a nice person, the motherly sort. On the whole the atmosphere in the house is good. If anyone's too much of a trouble-maker they're asked to leave by the outside committee which is responsible for all the basic management.

I don't think there's much else to say about the hostel, I can't think of anything else. I thought I'd fill you in on the background of it first, because if you meet someone you should give them as much information about where you come from as you can. If of course it was an outside person, someone I'd met in other circumstances, I wouldn't tell them I lived in a hostel for ex-offenders though, I'd say it was just an ordinary boarding house.

Turning to myself now, I was born in Catford in south London. My father worked as a shipping clerk in the docks. I never got very close to him, he was a person who always seemed very remote to me. He spent a lot of his time out of the house at evenings and weekends, down the pub with his mates. He'd been married before and either his wife had died or they were divorced, I don't know which. He had a son by her who was five years older than me: his name was Ron. Then I was the next one in age, then following me there was a girl and then another boy. My mother I'd say was an ordinary sort of person. She looked after us and kept us clean and fed. I'd say she was probably a kindly person too, although she never made much impact on me because she hardly spoke. She was quiet because I believe she suffered from some kind of nervous debility during most of her life but I don't know the medical name of it.

The person I remember most from my childhood and who I liked the best was my stepbrother Ron. He was in the RAF for a while, and when he came home on leave he was always very matey with me. He brought things for me as presents, and told me stories about what he'd been doing in Gibraltar and different places he'd been. He was very tall and good looking, and very confident and sure of himself. I've wondered sometimes if that was because of his training in the RAF. When he came out of the forces he joined an engineering company as a salesman. He was always smartly dressed and had a brand new car and in every way he was a success in life. I admired him because he always seemed to know what he wanted in life and how to get it. He went after it straight away and got it, that sort of person. He was also a big success with women, he had half a dozen girlfriends and each one was prettier than the last, and in the end he married the prettiest one of the lot and they bought a house in Wanstead. My father said to me once he thought Ron had a high potential for being a success because he had such a lot of go and drive in him, and I ought to try and be more like him. But I didn't have any go or drive myself. My father knew that and I knew that.

I went to a big secondary school where I wasn't a failure but I wasn't a star pupil either. I was somewhere around the top of the second stream all the time. Once or twice they experimented by putting me up into the top stream, but whenever they did I wasn't good enough for it and they moved me back down again. I wasn't particularly happy and I wasn't particularly unhappy as a schoolboy. I knew there wasn't much chance of me doing much academically, and I was hopeless at games and sports of every sort. From quite young I believed your future was out of your hands, your fate was determined when you were born and there was nothing you could do about it. I remember already as a schoolboy having the feeling that I'd been passed by, or a better way of putting it would be left on the shelf, if you can say that sort of thing about a schoolboy.

My first job when I left school was apprentice shop assistant with a chain of electrical shops. I had to go to different places and fill in for someone who was ill, then I'd be sent somewhere else the next week. I had various other small jobs of that sort with different firms, and the only thing of note I remember was that I had a very strong south London accent. I used to say 'wa-er' all the time instead of 'water', ''Ello 'ow's it goin' then?' and things like that. One of the firms I was with, when I left I asked them for a reference and they gave me a letter saying I was a reliable worker and time-keeper, but I wasn't suitable for anything where I had to come in contact with the general public, because I had such a terrible accent and half the time no one could understand what I said.

The main interest that I had in life was betting. Or to be truthful it wasn't my main interest, it was my only one. I used to go to the dog track two or three nights a week, at weekends I went to horse races, and in any spare time I had I went into betting shops. I lived at home and I didn't drink and sometimes I had good weeks and sometimes they were bad. If I had a good week and won a lot of money I didn't throw it around like some people do, showing off and buying presents for people. I just kept it and used it all up the next week on more gambling. I don't know if you've noticed it or come across it, but you nearly always find that people who are very keen on gambling are usually solitary and don't mix much.

I was like that, I didn't have any friends much at all. I was very shy with girls and never got anywhere with them. I'd ask one to go out for an evening and if she said yes, I'd take her to the dog track. Then the next time I asked they'd usually make an excuse, but if they did I wouldn't follow it up and say would they like to do something different, I'd leave it and not bother. I think girls found me what you'd call a lack-lustre person who never thought or talked much about anything but betting.

Another thing at that time, say seventeen or eighteen, was that I got very depressed a lot. I was always having headaches and pains in my chest, and palpitations. I was convinced I had something seriously wrong with me, and I went to different doctors and hospitals but whenever they examined me they always told me they couldn't find anything the matter. Sometimes they gave me tranquillizers or antidepressants, and at other times they said things like I shouldn't worry, or I should try and get more fresh air. There were also to a degree some sexual problems as well because I wasn't sure if I was homosexual or not.

I used to go up to Piccadilly Circus at night and walk about there to see if anyone fancied me and would try to pick me up. The first week I did it nothing happened, and then a middle aged man came up to me and asked me would I like to go to his flat with him. He was well spoken and well dressed and had a nice car, and he took me to quite a posh flat in Finchley. On the way he bought some Indian take-away food and a bottle of wine, and after we'd had the meal we had some brandy and he started showing me photographs of men and boys doing things together, and then we went to bed. The next day he let me stay at his flat all day while he went to work. He was obviously quite a well-off person, I think he was a solicitor, and I stayed with him for several days. He was very kind and gave me money to go out and buy shirts and a suit for myself; then after about three days he told me very politely that it was time for me to go.

I had quite a few experiences like that for about a year. I was then nineteen or twenty and quite good looking, and I enjoyed having some of the good things in life from such men. It wasn't actually prostitution because quite often there was no sex at all in it, all they wanted to do was talk to someone or play records and drink wine.

Up to that point I'd never done anything criminal. For instance if someone left me in their flat I wouldn't ever steal anything. But I did get interested in crime then, and tried one or two little burglaries and shopliftings. I also invented a way of forging betting-shop tickets to make it look as though I'd had a win. I never did it for a big enough sum of money to make it look suspicious though. All in all I had quite a nice little run of success for about nine months with the break-ins and the ticket winners. But then I got caught one night actually inside a betting shop I'd broken into to get a supply of tickets, and I was sent to prison for six months.

With remission I only had to do four months, and then the next milestone in my life was when I met a girl one day in a café. She wasn't working and she was on her own in a furnished room, and she was slightly mentally retarded. Her name was Lilian and I made her pregnant, and so she put pressure on me to marry her. At first I said no I wouldn't. She threatened to kill herself and I told her to go ahead, and she took a big overdose of aspirin. I think it was to try and frighten me, but as a result we did get married and we had our first child, a girl. We called her Julie, and through having her we were able to get a council flat in Norwood.

After we got married Lilian sort of began to grow on me. I'd only married her because I had to and I'd intended to drop her as soon as I could. But I got fond of her and she became pregnant again, although she was a very difficult person to live with. She was very materialistic like most women. If next door had a new washing-machine she had to have one, or a new colour telly and things like that. That was all right while we were living fairly comfortably on the proceeds of the little burglaries and robberies I was doing, but then I got caught again and this time I was sent to prison for fifteen months. Lilian had our second daughter Tracey while I was inside, and she had a difficult time financially. One time when she came on a visit she made me promise that when I came out I'd get a job and not do any more crime, and I said I would. It was more to keep her quiet and stop her nagging than anything else.

Then after I was released I started getting my headaches and chest pains again, as well as becoming depressed again. Lilian and I were quarrelling a lot, and I got very down and all my feelings about being a big failure kept coming back. One night I took a whole lot of pills together, tranquillizers and aspirins and antidepressants and I was taken to hospital in an ambulance to have my stomach pumped out. Afterwards I attended as an out-patient for a few months, and different doctors talked to me and said I should make an effort with myself, and try not think of myself as a failure all the time like I did.

Would you mind if we stopped there for tonight? We've covered a hell of a lot of ground and as we're now on the verge of where I did what I did, if you don't mind I'd sooner leave it there until next time.

He began talking without any preamble whatsoever next time, and continued in an uninterrupted monologue for forty minutes without any pause or prompting questions. His voice was expressionless except for one brief flurry of angrily intense swearing, which immediately afterwards subsided into a monotone again.

– Some of my suicide attempts were not all that serious, just overdoses of aspirin and things, cries for help they call them. But one or two of them were definitely serious. There are certain poisons you can buy that are weedkillers or there's another one for rats, and if you know where to go there are certain shopkeepers who don't ask you questions or make you sign forms. Lilian was definitely changing in her attitude as well. We'd been going on for several years with at times both of us out of work and both making suicide attempts. I could only get little jobs with very meagre pay because I was always having to stay off sick. She wouldn't let me try again at crime and see if I could do better at it, and we were always having rows and shouting at each other. She turned very cold and uncaring. She wasn't looking after the children properly either: sometimes she'd go out in the evenings drinking in the pub and not come home until late. Half the time I never knew where she was or who she was with. Children are very sensitive about these things, and I remember one night when I was putting her to bed, the eldest one Julie who was then eight said to me 'Daddy, how are things with you and Mummy?' I told her everything was fine and that all grown-ups had quarrels sometimes, but she looked at me as though she didn't believe me. Her younger sister Tracey was five and she was a much less worrying type of child, I don't think she was really aware of anything going on. Lilian decided that as I was off work sick so much, the best arrangement would be if I stayed at home permanently and looked after the kids, while she tried to get decent full-time work. She applied for a job training scheme to learn how to do management of works canteens, and it meant her going off to somewhere in Hertfordshire to a college and staying there Monday to Friday each week. She came home the first weekend, but then not the next one after that. She rang up a neighbour and left a message to say she'd got a lot of study work to do, and she was going to stay the weekend with a friend. She came home again the weekend after that, but I had the feeling she was concealing something from me and all she wanted to do was get back to Hertfordshire. All the time she was there we were quarrelling and Julie got very upset about it and cried. Next weekend there was another phone message to say she wasn't coming, this time because she hadn't enough money for the fare to get home. The weekend after that there was no word at all, she just didn't appear. So on the Monday I took the children to my mother and asked her to look after them for a couple of days, and then I went to Hertfordshire on the coach to find Lilian and have it out with her. At the town when I got off I enquired where the college was and started to walk there. Just as I was getting near it I saw her coming along towards me. She was walking with a man and they were laughing and joking. When they saw me he crossed over the road and disappeared down a street between some shops. When I got up to Lilian I really let her have it. I said to her I didn't care what she did herself, but she was making our children very unhappy by not being at home. I said they were the most important thing in the world to me, and I said 'If you go on hurting them, I'll fucking kill you I will and that's a promise.' I shouted at her in the street, I said 'You're a fucking disgrace you are, you ought to be fucking well ashamed of yourself.' I said 'I'm not having their lives fucked up like this, now you can fuck off you can, I'm having no more to fucking do with you.' I was full of anger and I turned round and went back to the bus station and caught the coach straight back to London. I didn't go round to my mother's to collect the children that night, I left it till the next day, then I went and brought them back to the flat. I told them I'd been to see their mummy and she'd sent them her love, everything was all right and she'd be coming home soon. The anger I had lasted about a day and then it began to change into sadness and depression, and I decided in the end the best thing to do would be to kill myself and our eldest daughter Julie, because that would be better for her than leaving her to Lilian who wouldn't look after her. I thought I'd kill her first, then I'd take Tracey the youngest one up to Hertfordshire on the coach and give her to her mother, then I'd come back home and kill myself. When Julie came home from school I gave her some jam sandwiches that I'd put a lot of crushed-up tranquillizer pills in, because I wanted her to be sleepy and not know what was happening to her. She ate all the sandwiches but they didn't seem to affect her. I told her to go and have a bath and get ready for bed, and I told Tracey to go out and play for a while. When she'd gone I went into the bathroom, and by then Julie did seem to be getting a bit sleepy, so I ended her life by pushing her head under the water and drowning her. When I was sure she was dead I let the water out and put a towel round her and lifted her out, and put her body in a cupboard on the landing, making sure it was out of sight behind some cardboard boxes and suitcases. When the little one Tracey came back from playing I told her there'd been a lovely surprise, her mummy had been and taken Julie away with her, and she was coming back again for her the next day. It was strange, because when I was talking to her I was being very cheerful about it but I was crying as well at the same time. I told her she should go and stay with my mother for the night, and I'd come and fetch her from school the next day. I took her to my mother's, and then when I was coming home I called in at a shop where I'd got things from before, and I bought a big packet of weedkiller poison. I mixed it up into a kind of dough and then put it on the kitchen table and shaped it like a cake and put it in a tin. I stayed up all night drinking coffee and taking pills. I didn't go and look at Julie's body in the cupboard, I sat at the kitchen table most of the time thinking about Tracey. My original idea had been to take her to Lilian in Hertfordshire, but the more I thought about it the more it seemed to me that wouldn't be a very good future for her. Then I had the idea I might give her to my mother to look after, but I thought that wouldn't work too well because my mother was getting on a bit in age and probably wouldn't be able to cope with her, and my father had died the year before. I went up to the school to collect Tracey the next afternoon, and on the way I saw a police car standing at the roadside. I decided I'd go and give myself up and tell them what I'd done, but as I was walking towards it it drove off. I picked up Tracey from school and brought her home, and she was very excited and asking me all the time if her mummy had come for her yet. When we got home I felt like a robot. And then the whole business happened all over again. I gave Tracey jam sandwiches with pills in them and when she'd eaten them she said she felt poorly, so I told her to go and have a bath and go to bed. But she didn't have a bath, all she wanted to do was to go to bed; she went and lay down, and when I went into the bedroom she was fast asleep. Unfortunately I then ended her life by smothering her with a pillow. When I knew she was definitely dead I went back into the kitchen and sat at the table and ate up all the weedkiller dough I'd made into a cake the night before. Then I went out and walked around for a while, and when I saw a phone box I rang up my doctor. I said I was sorry to have to say I'd got some sad news for him, I'd killed both my little daughters and I'd taken a lot of poison. He told me to go to the casualty department of the local hospital and get treatment for the poison, and said he'd come and meet me there. By then I was vomiting and feeling very ill. I thought the police would be waiting for me at the hospital but they weren't. I was put into intensive care and I thought they'd let me die because of what I'd done but they didn't. My doctor came, and then the police came, and they took me to a prison with a hospital wing, and much to my surprise after a few days I started to recover from the poison. A doctor who examined me in prison said I had a psychopathic disorder, with the result that at my trial it was said I had severely diminished responsibility and I wasn't fully responsible for my actions. So instead of being given a life sentence I was sent to Broadmoor under Section whatever it is of the Mental Health Act, which says you can be confined there for ever if necessary. I don't often talk as much as this and when I do I get very tired, so if you don't mind I'd like to stop again there and go on next time from that point.

— I was at Broadmoor first for three years, then I went to Rampton in Nottinghamshire, and then to Park Lane near Liverpool. All of them are what are called special hospitals, they're the responsibility of the Department of Health and not the Prison Service. They aren't very much different from prisons from what I've heard from people who've been in both, except the conditions are a bit more relaxed inside. But they're maximum security places and you're locked up. They're also very difficult to get out of in another way, insofar as with prisons you've either got a release date if you're doing a definite sentence, or if you're doing an indefinite one such as a life, there's a plan drawn up for you and it's designed to work towards a release date.

In the special hospitals you can be kept there for a much longer period of time. You'd be surprised how many people you meet in there who've been in them for twenty-five or thirty years or more, and have long since accepted they've no chance of ever going out ever. Some of them are old ladies and people like that, and some can't even remember what they were put there for in the first place. The staff aren't unkind to you, at least no one was ever particularly unkind to me, but you do feel you've been put away and forgotten about, and there's no one outside to care about you.

I felt this in my case because a year or so after I'd gone to Broadmoor my wife wrote asking me for a divorce, which I agreed to; and then not long after that I was notified that my mother had died. I don't know what's happened to my brothers and sister, it's many years since I've heard anything from them. I should think they probably don't want to have anything to do with me which you can understand.

For nearly all the three years I was at Broadmoor I had a plan of my own for myself, which was that I would kill myself when I got a suitable opportunity. I thought I'd save up the drugs they gave me until I'd got sufficient quantity to make sure it could be done. But I think they're wise to that sort of thing, and they either restrict the number they give you at a time, or they dispense them to you in liquid form so they can't be stored up. They also don't use drugs anything like as much as I thought they would: instead you have weekly interviews with doctors and therapists, and they encourage you to talk all the time about what's going on in your mind.

What they try to do mainly is give you an insight into your condition, so you'll be aware of the symptoms coming on, and go and ask for help if they do. One doctor told me I was what's called a depressive psychotic or a psychotic depressive, I can't remember which way round it is; two other doctors at different times said I was a psychopath. It was explained to me that a psychopath is someone who lacks the emotional feelings that other people have and this makes him act sometimes in an irresponsible way. Apparently there are two different kinds; aggressive psychopaths who go round with shotguns and weapons which they use for attacking people and committing armed robberies, and the other kind is inadequate psychopaths who lack feelings but can't cope with the world in general or do anything much to improve their situations.

They said the main cause of the disaster that happened in my life was because I couldn't deal with things that were getting on top of me. They also made me see how important it was that I should always go straight away to a psychiatric hospital whenever I had such feelings again, and tell them about myself and ask them to look after me. At first when they talked like that and asked questions to see if I understood properly what they were saying, I thought it might mean they were thinking of letting me out. They were very honest about it when I asked them though; they said in view of what had happened, they would have to be very careful in considering it, and not take any risks, which you can understand.

Moving me on from one hospital to another at about three-year intervals was more for a change of scenery for me than anything else. I don't recall there was any different kind of treatment between one and the other. Unlike if you're doing an ordinary life sentence, in a special hospital you don't get a release date as such at a time in the future. What you have to do is make an application yourself from time to time to a panel, and they consider your case. The first thing you have to apply for is to be given permission to go out for some half-day shopping trips. I was turned down twice for that in a year, and then they let me out accompanied by two of the staff. This was at Park Lane, and we went and looked round some of the big stores in Liverpool. You also get examined by visiting doctors who come, and they make reports separately on you to the panel.

For me it was altogether nine years before they agreed I could go on licence, but with a lot of conditions. One condition is I lived at an approved hostel which is what I'm doing, another that I see a psychiatrist once a week at the hospital here, and also that I see my probation officer once a week. So far, by the end of today, I shall have been out for fourteen weeks and ten days. I can be put back in a secure hospital at a moment's notice at any time.

Before long I hope to start trying to make a fresh start, but having all these appointments to see different people every week doesn't make it easy for me to get a job and settle down. I work when I can as a telephone salesman on a daily basis for a firm selling double glazing, but it's not very interesting and you're on commission only. It's a great big room with long desks in it, and people sit at them with a telephone and a pile of telephone directories. You pick out any number that you like, anywhere, and ring them up and ask them if they'd like a salesman to call. If they sound interested you write down their details, and if the end result's a sale, that's when you get some commission.

It's not a job with much future to it that I can see, so I look through the evening paper every lunch-time when it comes out in the hope I'll find something a bit better. If I could do that, then eventually I'd hope to move out of the hostel and live on my own if they'd let me, and perhaps have a bit more social life. So far I haven't made any friends at all outside. The people I meet at work are all there on a temporary basis, none of them stay long enough for you to get to know them. There was a girl there last week, when I went to a sandwich bar to get myself something for lunch she was there too and we walked back to work together. I asked her if we could meet after work for a drink one evening, and she said yes all right she wouldn't mind. Then she said she didn't know anything about me, and she'd like me to tell her something about myself. I don't know what made me do it, but I laughed and I said well I was a released murderer. A really funny look came over her face, so I laughed again and said of course I wasn't really, I'd only said it to scare her. But she said she didn't think she would come out with me after all. She left the job at the end of last week and she hasn't been there since. I expect I might have put her off. I was disappointed because I thought there might have been a chance of a bit of sex from her, which I would have liked.

The way I see things going on now is that the more time goes by, the better I shall get. I don't have depressions anything like as badly as I used to have, and if I do I know the doctor's there at the hospital and I ring up and make an appointment to see him. I always feel not as bad after I've talked with him. Three weeks ago I did something I've not done before, which is I went to the cemetery where my daughters are buried and looked at their grave. It upset me afterwards when I thought about it, but I came to the conclusion that on the whole it was the right thing for me to have done, to go and pay my respects as it were. I shall go again before long, and next time I'll perhaps take a bunch of flowers.

One thing I've always fancied doing when I can get round to it is that I've always thought I'd like to write a book. It'd be about Broadmoor and Rampton and Park Lane, and the strange people you meet in there; but mainly my own story, an autobiography, I've had a lot of experiences I could put in it. Well, I think a good title for it would be 'The Life and Times of an Inadequate Psychopath'.

SIX

A man with no history

ANDY REID

A small wiry slightly built man with a mop of thick curly black hair, he stood with his back to the room, looking out over the city rooftops from the tenth-floor window of the probation office, his hands buried deep in the pockets of his anorak, turning his head back over his shoulder when he spoke. His voice was gritty and deep, with a strong Glaswegian accent.

– There's no all that much to say to ye. I killed a man in a street, a stranger. Ah was walking along this road, a street off Sauchiehall Street, houses in it but no shops you know, a residential area like. Eleven o'clock at night, it's dark, and ah'm walking along minding ma own business. And I passed this man walking along in the same direction, I didna know who he was, ah'd never seen him before in all ma life. As ah go past him he says, almost in a whisper like you know, he says to me 'Oi oi' he says. I pulled out ma knife and I turned round and I stabbed him. I wasna so much trying to kill him ya know, ah was trying to hurt him, give him something to remember me by like. Ah don't know how many times I stabbed him altogether, but it was quite a few. Then I threw away ma knife, and I ran and ran.

That's all there is to it, there's no more ta tell ye about it than that. Because as for maself there's no hardly anything to say. I'm a man with no history. All ma life's been in custodial institutions, there's little else besides.

And I couldna talk to you here in a place like this: if you wanted ta talk you'd have to come to ma flat.

From a separate entrance under the steps to the front door, he had two rooms at the end of a dark basement corridor: they were bare-walled, undecorated and cheerless, and had scarcely any furniture in them apart from a single bed covered with a grey blanket, a cheap yellow plastic-topped kitchen table, two chairs and some small bookshelves crammed with wallet files and paperbacks.

On the fingers of one of his hands were tattooed the letters L O V E, and on those of the other one H A T E. Sometimes he intertwined them while he talked, sometimes they lay limply on his thighs. His words came out in staccato passages, followed by long silences while he brooded about what he'd said; sometimes he got up and walked about slowly, rubbing his neck and exercising its stiff muscles without speaking, then came back to his chair again and resumed his talking.

Subjects were rarely in sequence, nor were times and themes. On different evenings he'd begin on one subject, go on to another, then return to it the next day again. He started, stopped, repeated, reiterated, added, withdrew.

– I said ah was a man with no history didn'ah, and it's true. My history's all in ma dreams: terrible bad dreams I have. The night we'd met, after it I came home here and I couldna settle to eat or read a book or listen to the radio or anything, so I went over the road to the pub there and sat in a corner by maself all night and drank maself fuckin' stupid. What we'd been talkin' about, it was all still going on going round and round in ma head. Then ah came home an passed out there on the bed and didna wake up till three in the morning or mebbe half past and the light was still on. Christ I felt terrible. I'd wanted to avoid the bad dreams and it didna work, it never fucking does.

I ask myself what the fuck's best, talking about it and bringing it all back, or not talking about it an hoping one day it'll go away? It'll no go away if I talk about it and it'll no go away if I don't.

The bad dreams, they go on all the time too. Sometimes they seem like bad dreams about bad dreams, that's what they seem like. That's just what they're not though, believe you me. The bad dream that I have bad dreams about, that's not a dream that's reality that is, that I killed a man.

I haven't rehearsed before you've come or anything like that: I don't know what I'm going to say, I'm just going to let the words come out. I don't know if you'll understand any of it. I don't understand most of it myself. I'll make us some coffee first.

I'm thirty-five. I got my life sentence when I was eighteen and I did fourteen years. When I was a kid I was first put in an institution when I was eleven, I came out briefly, a few months, then I was put in another one when I was thirteen. That's fifteen years I've had in the outside world and twenty inside. The outside time was mostly in my young childhood so I don't remember a lot of that. The rest has been confinement: that's the only history I've got.

Because think of any ordinary man who's thirty-five. He's married, got a job, children, a house; he knows where he's been to get him where he is now, and he probably knows where he's going to from here. His past had a shape and his future's shaping up: to him and to other people, it all makes some kind of sense.

All I see though in my past's a hole, a black hole; an' in ma future an ever bigger and blacker hole still. Where I've been is nowhere, limbo: where I'm going towards is more of the same. I'm trying not to sound like a self-pitying person, because I'm not a self-pitying person: I'm clear sighted, I'm talking about fact. The future to most people is other people. I don't have any other people, I don't know any other people. Perhaps I don't want any other people, perhaps that's the fundamental fact. Perhaps that's why I don't see any difference between the past and the present. There's no noticeable difference between being in prison and now. The only difference I can see is when I was in prison I had to ask permission if I wanted to go for a shit. Now I can go when I want.

I was born in Falkirk but we moved to Glasgow when I was little. I expect it was to do with my father changing his job, he was an engineer of sorts, some kind of tool-maker; at least he was when he wasn't out of work and drinking or in gaol. He was only a petty criminal, nothing big or brilliant, either at crime or going straight. Most of his offences were for stealing or violence. Once he did time for assault on my mother; he and she separated several times and in the end they got divorced. I suppose at first they might have been happy together, at least they had five children: two girls and three boys, and I was the last. That was by the time they were quarrelling and fighting and separating: childhood for me was always unhappiness.

The only surprise to me is in the time it took before my mother eventually left him and went off with somebody else, and I've never seen or heard from her since. As for my father he might be alive or he might be dead now, I've not got the first idea.

It's easy to look back when you're older and say you did something because of something. Me, I broke into the gas meter in a neighbour's house; I've told lots of people in my time it was because I wanted money to run away to London with, to get away from the home atmosphere. I don't really know whether it was or it was not. When you're an eleven-year-old kid and all your pals are all the time doing the same thing, you don't have to have a reason for breaking into a gas meter. You do it because it's exciting and you're proving you're just as brave as everyone else. There's a prison phrase about petty criminals, they're only gas-meter bandits: there's some truth in that with kids, you're all bandits together, outlaws.

I would say the first time I was sent to approved school, I was told it was for my own good. That was right too: in many ways it was. I was happier at approved school than I had been at home. The main reason for it was there wasn't so much violence there, people talked to you instead of giving you a belting all the time, which was how it had been at home.

The only rule in our home was fear: fear of pain and

violence. It was just endless. Endless and senseless: depending entirely on how my father was feeling, not on anything any of us had done. He wasn't a big man physically, though he seemed like he was to me as a kid. But he was a totally violent man when he was sober, and a totally even more violent man when he was drunk. The only reaction he knew to anything was to hit out and keep on hitting. My mother, my brothers and sisters; and most often because I was the littlest one, me. Two incidents I remember in particular were once when he thrashed me for something I'd done or not done, whichever it was, with a thick studded belt he wore with brass points on. I was about eight. And another time I remember when he went and got the dog chain hanging up by the kitchen door, and laid into me with that. The times he hit with his fists, or kicked my legs and hard, I don't remember any of them as memorable. That was his normal behaviour all the time. I can put my feelings about him very simply: I hated him.

The second time I was sent to approved school was at thirteen, and it was for another breaking-in and stealing money, I think that time it might have been a shop. It was a tougher place and I was definitely a tough kid by then all right; and when I got there, I made sure I immediately established a reputation. I had to, because I was small; if I didn't I would have been picked out and picked on. I had to show I was more ready for a fight than anyone else was, big or small. I cultivated what they call a short fuse: the moment anybody said anything to me, even if they meant it innocently, I'd take it the wrong way, on purpose, and go at them with my fists. Show you've a quick temper, let everyone know you've got it, they'd better not take the smallest liberty. If they do they'll have a fight on their hands. That's the only way you survive. Show you can fight and give pain. And take pain too. Once I remember I smashed my fist through a window pane. You always got homosexual advances made to you if you were small like I was and not tough looking. It used to disgust me, I got absolutely wild that someone should think I was like that, so I smashed my fist through the glass to show I wasn't.

– The second approved school's atmosphere was it was a place where even as regards the staff, the only principle it had was violence. You didn't have a lot of schooling there, you didn't get much education. Least not in the acceptable scholarly subjects. It was run by the Christian Brothers, a gang of big brutal men almost without exception, terrorists in the real sense of the word: they ruled by terrorizing. Anything you said or did that was out of place – and they were the ones who decided what was in place and what wasn't – and they came down on you in a mob, whacking you with sticks, punching you with fists, slashing you with straps. There was one Brother called Slogger, because wherever he went he always carried a cricket bat. I never saw him put it to use on a cricket field, but he was perpetually swiping you on your backside. He'd do it just for the enjoyment of it if he ever came up on you from behind. I don't know what he called his religion, but his driving force was something called sadism. He was the sort if you did something wrong and he found out, he was almost pleased by it. A gleam of anticipation'd come in his eye at the prospect of caning or beating you for it.

After approved school, I came down south to England. Glasgow was no good, my mother was off one place and my father another. London's the only idea runaway Scots boys have in their heads. Streets paved with gold, they really think of it in those terms. Within days I'd met up with some lads who were making a living in a variety of ways, none of which was legal. They were outside society: individualists, anarchists, free people in themselves. Their way of life didn't suit me. It wasn't the criminal aspects, they didn't worry me: it was the unstructured part of it, the way you took things one at a time, whatever came next. At an early impressionable age I'd had a structured lifestyle: in approved schools, and if someone as young as that can be institutionalized, then I was.

So naturally my thoughts turned to the Army. In those days it wasn't like now when they're more choosy, they'd take almost anyone. I only lasted eight months, and for five of those I was in the glasshouse for fighting. In the Army you're supposed to keep your aggressive instincts to let loose on the enemy. I didn't do that: I never got near an enemy, I was busy fighting other soldiers or anyone else that happened to be there. I was ready to start a fight at any kind of an insult, real or imaginary: someone only needed to look at me and I'd be questioning them why they were looking at me that way, were they looking for a fight? There was something a bit wrong with me, I think there's no question of that.

I had three months in an Army barracks, supposed to be basic squaddie training. Some lads went to their homes for weekends: not me because I didn't have one. The high spot of the week was Saturday night, into civvies and down into town with a few of the others and into the pubs. The ones we weren't barred from got very few, but there was always somewhere'd serve you a drink. I think there was a place called the King's Head, a real notorious place where you could get anything you wanted: drink, drugs, tarts, whatever you liked. One Saturday night there was this big bloke standing up at the bar, and he was doing the thing I liked least, which was looking at me. I went up to him and gave him my usual form of greeting: which was to ask him what was he looking at, was he looking for a fight? He answered me with cheek: he said 'Be very careful sonny, I'm a policeman, I can look at anyone I like.' Patting me on the head, almost, the tone in his voice. So I said to him 'Ha fucking ha'; and I took hold of his beer bottle on the counter in front of him, and I brought it down with a whack on his head. It smashed, glass everywhere, cut him all over the head and face and neck. Grievous bodily harm they called it: that was what the charge was, there was no way they were going to reduce it in return for a plea. And that was what they got, because it was true, he was a policeman. They don't like that, so it was six months in a detention centre and discharged from the Army.

Aye, so much for my military career. I'll make us a cup of coffee.

— Violence. I was thinking about it afterwards the other night. Either you understand it or you don't. If you understand it, you find it hard to explain to somebody who doesn't. You've never questioned it, you've always taken it for granted, part and parcel of everyday life. It's normal: what would be abnormal would be if violence wasn't in your life.

I was brought up with it, I was brought up to it. My father carried a knife, my brothers carried knives, everyone: you wore a shirt and trousers and shoes, and a knife. You weren't properly dressed without one. When you were arrested and searched, the Law knew what they were looking for, it was always there. It wasn't usually hidden, so if they didn't find it that made them suspicious. They couldn't ask their question then that they always ask: 'What's this, why'd you carry a knife?' A stupid question, but you always gave the sensible answer: 'Because I always carry a knife.' 'Always?' 'Always.' 'Why?' Here we go round again. 'Because I always do, I always carry a knife.'

And they always have you for it: in law carrying a knife is premeditation. They call it 'a weapon of offence'. Mark that: offence, not defence. You carry a knife for protection, but they won't have that: you're premeditating attacking somebody.

Before, I stopped at the DC. Now that is violence, real violence a detention centre is. They do things to you at a detention centre, mentally and physically, as bad or worse than anything you could have got sent there for in the first place. Beatings, kickings, humiliations: they heap them on you one on top of another. The idea's to break your spirit, to show you violence doesn't pay, that if you give it out you'll get it back ten times over. So what do you learn? If you haven't got it already, you learn hatred of authority and determination you're not going to let it break your spirit. You're not going to let it win, you're going to show them you're stronger and tougher than they are. If you don't, you go under. You come out looking back on it with pride. They didn't break me. I won, I won. It's like graduating from an academy, it's a great feeling. Stay violent you say to yourself: stay violent and you'll win out in the end. You come out bitter at them and what they tried to do, but proud because you didn't let them. You could really call yourself a fully fledged hard man.

I went back to Glasgow as that, after the DC. Temporarily I went back home, because temporarily there was one. My father and mother were having one of their periodic reconciliations. It was the first time my father'd ever been proud of me: I'd grown up like him and my brothers into a hard man. That was the greatest thing in the world you could be. There was nothing he liked better than when we could all be got together of an evening, and go down the pubs looking for trouble. 'Let's go see if we can find Jocky Campbell' he'd say; and off we'd go looking for Jocky Campbell. If we were lucky and he was unlucky we found him. When we did we'd beat him up, with any of his friends who wanted to join in. He didn't need to have done anything, all he needed was to be Jocky Campbell. There was nothing my father liked better than to walk into a bar, a hard man with his three hard sons behind him, and ask in a loud voice for Jocky or whoever else he'd in mind at the time. If they weren't there, a swift pint and then on to the next pub.

I'm talking about violence and trying to give a picture of it. I said I hated my father, and I did: more every time I saw him. My violence didn't love his violence: it hated it. I suppose it must sound strange.

— It was an old con in prison first sussed me out. Some of those old men in there, they'd spent nearly their whole lives in prison doing long sentences. They'd be out for a few months, maybe a couple of years, then get caught and be back inside. They'd have started their lives of crime when they were young, perhaps in their twenties; and you'd meet them and go on meeting them, each different prison you were sent to, when they were forty, fifty, sixty, doing maybe another ten years. They were big men quite a few of them, I mean big in crime, household names almost. Sort of professors in university. If you wanted to learn about crime you could learn everything from them. If you wanted to learn how to survive in prison that was another thing you could learn. They were men of standing, they had brains.

My first six or seven years inside after my life sentence I was fighting for survival. Literally fighting, the same as I had done in approved school and detention centre. Keeping up the hard image, fighting with the other cons and then fighting with the screws who came to sort it out.

They can't punish a lifer by docking his remission, he hasn't got a release date. So what they do instead's not put you up for consideration by the Parole Board: they delay it and delay it until you start behaving yourself. That's what happened with me: on average a lifer'll do seven eight nine years, something in that order. Well I did fourteen. It wasn't because my crime was all that bad compared with others: what was bad was my behaviour. I was kept as a Category A prisoner for seven and a half years: that's one they consider a high security risk, someone who'd be a danger to society if he ever escaped. I was a danger to society all right, no argument about that. But not to outside society, to the fabric of prison society inside.

The screws, a lot of them were pure bastards, sadists many of them were. What sort of a man does what they do, get job satisfaction from keeping his fellow human beings locked up? They enjoyed winding people like me up. They knew they could provoke me into fighting and they did. A whisper here about what some other prisoner'd said, a word there about how I should watch out for another screw because he'd got it in for me. Either of them, both of them,

I'd go after them, find them and front them up. Then as soon as the fighting started, twenty screws or more'd come running, batter me and carry me off to solitary confinement.

What started ma telling you this? Oh aye the old con. He was a man then about sixty I suppose: he'd done a long long time and he was still going to do a long time more. Years back he'd killed a policeman, and they don't like that: you'll do longer for killing a policeman than for anything else there is. I'd been down on punishment for the tenth time or however many it was, and he took me aside one day and told me authority was beating me. I said to him 'Fuck off you silly cunt, that's just what they're not doing and I'm showing them they're not.' 'They are' he said, 'they are: you'll never beat the prison system that way, it's too big too powerful too strong. They can go on doing it to you for as long as they want; and if you let them go on doing it, they will.'

There was something about the way he was talking, quietly, fatherly: he said to me 'Now sit down Andy and let's talk about it.' He said he'd done more time than my age was; he knew all there was to know and a lot more besides. He'd seen men like me before, the screws had them marked down as fair game to wind up, and they enjoyed doing it a lot of them. That was fair enough, that was clear enough, I'd seen it, I knew it myself. The way I was doing my sentence, he said to me, was the hardest way there was. And what was I doing it for? What was I trying to prove, that they weren't going to beat me? What I was proving was they were. And then he said, I remember his words exactly: he said 'You know Andy, going on behaving like you are, you're giving yourself no sort of a life son at all.'

I burst out laughing. Doing a life sentence and being told I was doing no sort of a life. I thought it was the funniest thing anyone'd ever said to me.

Only those words sank in they did. They stayed in my head, they made me think. We talked a few times more, and he said things like there was nothing to get out of a life sentence except what you put into it. The options you had

as to what you could put into it were strictly limited; but
there were a few things you could do if you had a mind to.
'Oh yes such as what?' 'Study.' 'Study, me?' 'Yes, study,
you.' I gave him my usual response, a foul-mouthed
slagging-off. Then the next day he came round to it again.
And the next.

I'm out of cigarette tobacco, I canna talk without ma
smokes, I've got to stop and go out and get some.

– Prison culture, it dominates you, it's all around you. Some
guys in prison, they climb up on chairs and tables in the
cells and look out through the bars at what they can see of
the outside world. And they talk of it and talk of it, but it's
never anything else but fantasies and dreams. 'When I get
out, when I get out. When I get out I'm going to get drunk
every night of the week and twice on Sundays. When I get
out whatever I do or don't do, there's one thing I'm going to
make certain of and that's that I have a really good long fuck
every night. When I get out I'm going to graft really hard,
no small stuff: I reckon if I can pull one good job a month
steady, that'll give me all I need. Only this time I'm going to
be clever about it, I'm not going to do impulse stuff, I'm
going to plan every little detail, be dead certain I don't get
caught. When I get out, when I get out.'

There's no point a lifer doing any of that. Least there
wasn't for me. I wasn't ever going to get out, outside was a
fantasy wasn't worth wasting the time thinking about.
'When I'm free': it was just a phrase. I was in for life. I'm
not outside now, I'm still inside, in my head. What does it
mean, outside? What it means to me is only that I'm in the
outside life. I'm in it but I'm not of it, I'm outside physically but mentally I'm still inside. It's only like they tell
you, licensed release. Not after-care: after-control. You're
still under someone's control, your probation officer can
pull you back inside any time he wants to. He lets you know
it, it's there all the time hanging over you. He has your
address and if you move you've got to have his permission

first, notify him of your new address as soon as you get there. The police have it too: everything about you, it's all on their computer. Any murder or suspicious death in a five-mile radius of where you are and it's automatic, you're the first person they come round to see. 'Where were you last night, Andy? Never mind asking us why'd we want to know, we're the ones who ask the questions. Where were you last night Andy? Oh yeah, can you prove that to us? You went to the cinema, where did you sit, what time did the main film start? What else was on, what else did you see? How much did you pay for your ticket? How did you get there, how much was the fare? Now don't start getting stroppy about it Andy, we're your friends, we're only asking you these questions so we can put you in the clear straight off.'

'Straight off'. That confirms it, you were the first one they came to see. 'We're your friends'. The laugh about that is before long you start to believe it, you do. You think, Yes that's right, yes they are my friends, they're the ones who know all about me. I don't have any other friends or acquaintances who do that, the police are the only ones who know all about me that there is to know. Yes right, they are my friends, my only friends. It's not exactly a two-way relationship though. They only come to see you when they think they might be able to have you for something, they don't ever drop in just to see how you're doing and pass the time of day. Your friends are your enemies, your enemies are your friends. It's like here on my fingers that I had done in the DC: love and hate, they go together, yin and yang.

– My biggest difficulty, it's living with myself, trying to come to terms with myself, face what I've done. I took someone's life away; because I didn't like the tone of his voice, no more reason than that. Whatever he was, whoever he was, he hadn't gone out expecting to get slaughtered for just saying something to someone as they walked past him in the street. There's no way I can give him his life back or make restitution. I used to think in prison because of that there was no point in me being released. There was nothing I could do to give myself back any worth. What I'd done was final, irrevocable, and it wasn't done for any even faintly acceptable reason. Murder for gain, people can understand that. Or murder in war, something depersonalized, they even invest that with a kind of heroism. You die for your country, you kill for your country. That's very acceptable indeed, you get medals for it and handclapping and cheers. You've killed people for no reason other than you've been told to, your political leaders tell you it's a good thing and they want it done. Not what I did though, you don't get medals or cheers for that. So where's the reality? I can't connect it up. It makes no sense. I relive it time after time and it still makes no sense. I don't make excuses for it, I wouldn't even think of talking excuses; I never have. There's good murders and there's bad murders, and this was one of the very worst.

It was late at night when I was walking along this street. I passed this man, I didn't know him, and just for a moment I couldn't believe what had happened. As I went past him he put his hand out and he patted me on the bum. And then he called after me, very softly, it was like invitingly, he called out 'Oi oi.' I can't stand things like that, I was wearing my knife and I turned round and stabbed him and went on stabbing him. I'm not saying I said it aloud, I don't remember that I did; but the phrase I was saying inside my head was 'I'll kill you I will, I'll kill you.' People do say that. Out loud or inside their head. But not usually when they have a knife in their hand and are actually doing it.

I went back to where I was staying, I was staying with a relative or a friend. Actually she was both, she was the mother-in-law of one of my brothers. I'd been running, I was breathless, I was shocked. She asked me what had happened and I told her, and she asked me did I want her to send for the police. I said no I didn't, not yet, and she made me a cup of tea. Then I said I was ready: but she didn't need to send for them, I went to them myself.

– What that old con had said to me, he'd said read, better myself, study, I'd got a brain, use it, think about something else other than all the time trying to demonstrate how tough I was. That was undemonstrable anyway, and not worth doing either.

I wasn't scared of anyone or anything I thought. I was at first though, I was scared of books. Textbooks with knowledge inside them: I found them frightening things. I went and asked the Education Officer in the prison, I'll never forget the look on his face. 'I want to study.' 'You want to study Andy, you?' 'Yes me, I want to study.' 'What do you want to study?' 'How the fuck do I know what I want to study, what sort of things do people study?' 'You're sure you want to study?' 'Yes of course I'm fucking sure.' One more line of it and I've have walked out of his office.

So I studied. I studied English literature and English language, and I studied psychology and sociology and maths. Books didn't frighten me any more, I read E. M. Forster, Aldous Huxley, Bertrand Russell, Jung, people like that. I stopped fighting and I started learning how to put it all to work, all that fierceness and energy and force. I'd stay up all night reading: you'd get the odd landing screw now and again who'd be decent enough to let you keep your cell light on. It got like I was hooked on a drug, reading and learning: the more you have, the more you need. The education department fixed me up with an O-level correspondence course, and in the end I got five.

Then I moved to another prison and I was lucky there, the education department was even better still. I got into full-time education instead of working in the laundry, and took literature and sociology further on and got A levels in both of them.

They encouraged me to put in for a provisional place at a polytechnic for when I came out. When you don't have a release date, I don't think they take you seriously when you apply. I tried this one and that one but never got anywhere; the nearest I've got so far is a provisional place for next year if I can keep myself going financially till then. So I do casual work, labouring, driving, anything, and wait. I don't want to let the study go if I can help it and there's chance of a grant. There's no more I can do than wait. But I'm not optimistic about it, the future's never been something that's had much reality or meaning for me. What I'd like to do is study psychology; but to use it when or where or for what I don't know, I don't even think about that far ahead.

When it happened, it was one of the times when my father and mother were back together again. I wasn't living in their house, I was living at the house of a friend or relative: a series of places temporarily, anywhere that'd take me so long as I could get away from the fighting and quarrelling all the time going on with my father and mother. I'd gone round the night before to see them: my father'd been drinking as usual, and him and me we had a big row, he accused me of stealing money from him. I hadn't. I was angry with him, I went round to the house again the next night to have it out with him. It was late on, I'd had a few drinks maself in a pub before I went. When I got there he'd gone out, my mother said he'd be in some pub or other, it'd be late when he got back so there was no point me stopping waiting for him. She knew there'd be another big quarrel between us if I was there when he came back. She wanted me out of the house. She kept telling me not to stay but to go. In the end I said all right I would, and I went. I didn't tell her it was frustration, I was only going to go out and look for him, I knew the pubs he drank in, I knew I'd find him in one or other of them. I wanted to find him, I wanted to do him harm.

It was late at night and I was walking along this street. As I passed this guy he said 'Oi oi' and touched me, and I turned round and stabbed him. I was looking for ma father really. It all keeps going round and round in ma head.

SEVEN

You do still wonder sometimes

VALERIE SCOTT

A hot afternoon in summer; laughter from a children's play area below floated up through the open window of her seventh-floor south London council flat. Small, dark haired and green eyed, in a grey pleated skirt and a crisp white blouse, she cleared her throat nervously from time to time as she talked. On a low table a tray with a freshly ironed cloth, unmatching cups and saucers and a plate with six biscuits.

– Do you mind if I smoke? I'll give it up one day. Everyone says that don't they? It's ridiculous, I spend more on cigarettes than food. I don't drink though so I suppose that's something. I worked out last week that if I don't smoke for a fortnight, I could buy a nice piece of carpet for this room that I saw in a shop in the High Street. And another fortnight after that a sofa a bloke's got in his second-hand furniture shop over the other side of the estate.

Gradually bit by bit I'll get it looking more presentable and try to give it some character. It looks impermanent doesn't it? It is: I'm not going to stop here longer than I have to. It does have advantages though: this whole estate's like a rabbit warren you can lose yourself in. Nobody knows who you are, where you've come from or where you're going to. Nobody notices you. It can be lonely but I'd sooner it was like that, I can keep myself to myself until I get things more sorted out about what I'm going to do.

I did eleven years in prison and I came out six months ago at the age of forty-one. I'm very bitter about this that I'm going to tell you, but I'd sooner say it at the beginning, otherwise it'll be hanging over me until it's said. I thought forty-one, that's not too late to start making a new life for yourself; and before not long, only a few weeks, I saw an advert in a magazine for a live-in cook-housekeeper wanted for an elderly couple not far from here. I thought that'd be good, just what I wanted: somewhere to live, all found and a bit of pocket money on top.

I wrote after it, and a week later I got a reply not from the couple, but from their daughter and her husband, asking me to go and be interviewed. They explained to me they didn't want to put the parents into an old people's home because they could still look after themselves to an extent; but they'd be happier if there was someone there with them all the time, to do most of their cooking and housework. They didn't ask too many awkward questions: I told them I'd been abroad and come back because my marriage had broken up, and I wanted to start a new life. They said would I go and see the old couple: and if they were satisfied with me, and I was satisfied with them and their house and what accommodation they'd offer me for my own use, then I could start on the basis of a two-month trial. The wife was a bit anxious: her mother could be very cranky and difficult she said, and they'd had a lot of trouble finding people who could put up with her and would stay.

I went along and the old couple were fine, I liked them and they seemed to like me too; they showed me where I'd have my own comfortable little bed-sitting room with a colour TV, my own kitchenette and toilet and everything, I couldn't believe my luck. Having only just come out of prison and reporting to my probation officer twice a week, I could see there was going to be no problem about that: I had time off every day so I could go over to see her on the bus. I told her about it before I started, what my address would be and all the rest of it, and she raised no objection at all.

So I began the job. It was true the old lady could be a bit difficult at times if things weren't exactly as she liked them, but that was no strain for me, particularly after some of the types you meet in prison, I can tell you. And it was the old lady herself, before we even got to the end of the two-month trial period, who asked me if I'd stay on on a permanent basis.

But when I went back and told my probation officer about it, she absolutely took my breath away. She said if it was going to be permanent, I had to tell the daughter and her husband, who were the ones who were officially my employers, about my background: that I was a lifer who'd done eleven years for murder and was out on licence. I went absolutely potty. I said what the hell had that got to do with the job, I wasn't a thief, I'd no convictions for stealing or dishonesty, why the hell did they have to be told? But she insisted: she said I'd no choice, I had to tell them, and what's more she was going to check with them a week later that I had told them.

I felt so sick I can't describe it. I rang the daughter up and said could I go round and see her, there was something had come up that I had to talk to her about. The first thing she said was 'Oh God, has mother been playing up again?' I said no it wasn't that, it was something I had to tell her, but it wasn't something I wanted to say over the phone. She was on her own when I got to her house; she invited me in and to sit down. I took a deep breath and then I said 'I'm under the supervision of a probation officer, and she insists that I have to give you some information.' She was very nice, she smiled, and she said well lots of people were on probation, what'd I done? I said no, I wasn't on probation, I was on parole. Like most people she didn't know the difference: she asked what did that mean? I said well I'd been in prison for a long time on a life sentence. And then that was it, I had to say what for: that I'd committed a murder. I'd killed someone and I was only released on licence.

I could see from her face it shook her all right. She said she obviously couldn't take a decision herself, she'd have to talk it over with her husband when he came home in the evening: I should ring them up about nine o'clock and they'd give me their answer. As I was going out of the door she sounded really upset, she said 'Oh God, what did you have to tell me for?' I rang up at nine o'clock: and she sounded very sad but she said they had to think of the old people first, and on balance they'd decided if the probation people had made me tell them, that meant there must be a good reason for it. So they were very sorry, they didn't feel they could keep me on; but they'd pay me a month's extra salary and give me a good work reference any time I wanted one.

Since then I've had a part-time job that lasted two weeks at a hamburger take-away, then I was off with a bad cold for four days and they told me not to bother going back; then a waitress for a week, and a barmaid for two nights that I walked out of because I hate pubs and men trying to chat you up and telling you dirty jokes all the time. Apart from that, nothing; and I live like I am now, on Social Security. The probation really wrecked things for me, that's what I feel. I had my own job, my own nice little place, I worked hard and put up with the old lady's funny little ways: and they completely fucked it all up.

– I murdered my best friend, a girl called Sandra, when I was twenty-nine. She and I were sharing a flat together, and we were both working for the same bloke, a man called Michael. He was my boyfriend, and I discovered he'd been going with her behind my back. I was a very jealous person, very quick tempered, and though I'm small and don't look it, I was physically very strong. I fronted up Sandra about what was going on but she only laughed at me and taunted me. I just boiled over with rage: I killed her with my bare hands, I punched her in the throat and strangled her. After I'd done it I was terrified, and I went and gave myself up at the police station. It sounds a funny thing to say, but while I was in Holloway on remand waiting for my trial, the only person I kept hoping would come and visit me was Sandra, I missed her very much.

Michael of course didn't put in an appearance. I suppose he had about six or eight other girls working for him, and for his own personal girlfriend he replaced me with one of them. I've never seen him since from that day on. A lot of people find it hard to understand how you can love a man who puts you out to work like he did me; but I did love him, I was crazy about him. I'd had a hard life and a tough one, and I was hard and tough on the outside, very. But like anyone else I needed love and affection, and in his own way that was what he gave me, even if he shared it around with one or two others. I've had a lot of time in the last eleven years to think about that period of my life between say twenty and twenty-nine, and I still can't properly sort out why my feelings for him were so strong. But strong they were, they were so strong I killed Sandra because of him; and that's something I can't get away from, ever.

My mother told me once I'd always been bad tempered and violent right from when I was little. My early life I only know bits and pieces about, because she and my father were divorced before I was born. I don't know if it's true or not, but she told me in those days that about the only way you could get a divorce was on grounds of the wife's adultery, so she went to a hotel for a night with a man. According to her, the man wasn't someone she knew well and she only went with him once; but it was on that night that I was conceived. She said she didn't even know his name so she couldn't ever tell me anything about my father: all she could remember was she cried and cried when she found she was pregnant. She never wanted me and she never pretended she did: she put me in a series of children's homes until I was sixteen. By then she was married to someone else; she told me to my face I was old enough to make my own way in the world, and that's what I'd have to do.

This was down in Kent: Herne Bay, somewhere around there. I went and worked in a hospital as a domestic, and lived in a hostel they had for girls. I was very ignorant and innocent, and I had sex with the first boyfriend I ever had, and got pregnant. I wasn't yet seventeen when I had a baby daughter, but I had to move out of the hostel into a furnished room because of her. I called her Adele. It was very hard for a girl as young as I was trying to look after a little baby on her own only a few months old. The boy who was Adele's father didn't want to know about her, or about me.

But one day his elder sister came to see me. She said she and her husband wanted to have children but couldn't. And she said that if I ever found I really couldn't manage, she'd be happy to have Adele and they'd bring her up as their own. The husband had a decent job, and they had a nice house; so one day when I was really down and depressed, I went in a call box and phoned them up and said if they wanted Adele they could have her, only they'd have to come and get her there and then before I changed my mind.

They were round in their car in less than half an hour. I gave Adele to them, and I've never set eyes on her since. At first I used to ring them up from time to time to ask how she was getting on with them, but then I didn't do it any more. Not long afterwards the husband moved to a new job somewhere up north, and we gradually lost contact; I've not heard anything about them or where they are for years. I wouldn't want to see her again now; I'm sure she's had a better life with them than I could have given her.

After she'd gone, I had a reaction and went sort of half crazy. I'd go with any man who asked me, and in the end like a lot of young girls I drifted up to London and the West End. I lived a pretty terrible sort of life; about the only good thing I can say for myself was I was never into using drugs. Then after a year or two I met Michael, and I've told you the rest. It's not a period to look back on with any happiness or pride; though there isn't any period in my life at all I could say there was, at all.

And you know, there's still this rankling feeling inside me I was telling you about last time, that business with the housekeeper-companion job and how I was forced into the position where I lost it. I suppose I might be pulling the wool over my own eyes, but I honestly really did feel I'd got a terrific chance of making a completely fresh start in my life then. What's more, it was just at a time when I really wanted to do it. There's two sorts of people you meet in prison: those who can't wait to get back to what they think are the bright lights and glamour and excitement: usually they're the younger ones, who've still not seen sense about how they're wasting their lives. And the other kind are those who've grown up and matured a bit: they've realized there's more to life than cars and money and excitement. All they want's a bit of peace and quiet and the chance to make life have some meaning. That was how I was when I came out, definitely. So when something happens like's just happened to me, you can't help feeling Well is it worth it to even try any more? That's not a good state of mind to be in, not at all.

There's one other thing too that you've got hanging over your head, when you've done something like I did. It's there all the time, that great big question mark: have I changed? When I committed murder, there's only one word for it, I was ferocious. After it, all through the first five or six years I was in prison, I stayed like that: I was a right bastard, I really was. I never stopped to think: if someone crossed me, I lashed out. It didn't matter whether they were big or small, a screw or a prisoner, I'd attack them and keep on attacking them until I was flat on the floor from the sheer weight of numbers of officers holding me down. I saw doctors, psychologists, psychiatrists time after time, and they all always told me the same thing: Control yourself Val, learn to control yourself or you'll never get out. I didn't need them to tell me, I knew it myself already: what I didn't know and they couldn't tell me either, was how?

It did happen eventually, I don't know how or why. As I got into the second half of my thirties, I did find that somehow I was starting to simmer down, or I thought I was. I still effed and blinded with the best of them, but I began to be a lot less ready to lash out physically. I recognized the change, and the prison people did too: that was how in the end they gave me a date for my release eighteen months ahead, on condition I gave them no more trouble. Which I didn't: I'd conquered whatever it was in me, I'd taught myself how to behave like a rational person at last. Well as I say as I thought.

And then: well. Perhaps it was losing the live-in job that upset me or what, I don't know. But two weeks last Friday I was in the local supermarket in the High Street here, pushing my trolley round and looking at the shelves, and a young black lad made a grab at my handbag. He didn't get it; but I swung round on him and gave him a kick on his shins so hard I should think he's probably only just now starting to hobble around again. Only you know, afterwards, I came back here and I sat down in that chair, and I was shaking and shaking and couldn't stop.

I'd done it again. After all these years that I'd been telling myself I never would any more, I'd lashed out; and for something as unimportant as that. It makes you realize that whatever it was was inside you, it hasn't gone. So when will the next time be? What will it be about, and what'll happen? You can't help it; but you do still wonder sometimes.

Where I'll go now from here I don't know. Towards the end of my time inside I did some training in office working, typing, telephone receptionist, that sort of thing. It's sketchy naturally, it has to be, and there's always the problem you have to say where you studied and how you got your certificates, and why you haven't got any actual experience except in Holloway, Styal women's prison and Askham Grange. You have to give the game away straight away. If you don't, the Probation Service'll give it away for you. You almost feel you're on the scrap heap before you start.

So the honest answer is I don't know where I'll go and I don't know what I'll do. I don't know anyone, and no one knows me. On this estate I live like a secret person, and that's how I like to be. In prison I decided crime wasn't something I fancied turning my hand to, not just like that; most women criminals, they're at it at one remove if you know what I mean. They live with a man who's into it, looking after him but not actually doing anything much themselves. Well I can't see myself doing that, because I don't like men: not any men of any kind. I don't mean I'm lesbian because I'm not; if you're interested in it there's plenty of opportunity in prison but it never appealed to me, not once in eleven years. But the idea of living with a man or even marrying one, now, at my age, that doesn't appeal either. You'd have to tie yourself down, and most probably to the sort of person you're trying to keep away from. So I can't see it happening, there's no way it could, I wouldn't let it. I might be unsure of everything else, but one thing I do know is that no, marriage definitely isn't for me: oh no no, definitely not.

She lit another cigarette, drew on it hard and stared into the future, her face set.

On a sunny Saturday morning four years later, the church congregation of sixty rhythmically clapped their hands and stamped their feet in unison as they sang an exuberant rendering of 'Yes, Jesus Loves Me Evermore', accompanied by a young four-piece group of two guitarists, a saxophonist and a keyboard player. Arms raised in celebration she came skipping back down the aisle in her bright floral print dress, through the kisses and embraces and handshakes of her friends. Less demonstratively her smiling husband walked behind her: a slim man of fifty, bespectacled, hair greying, in a tailor-neat dark suit with a pale blue shirt and burgundy tie.

A week afterwards, she put down the gilt tea tray with its embroidered cloth and its matching cups, saucers, cream jug and sugar bowl, and leaned contentedly back in one of the two armchairs in the light airy sitting-room of their small first-floor maisonette.

– Oh yes I remember, of course I do. It was something along the lines of 'No no, I'll never get married, oh no' wasn't that it? So it just shows doesn't it, how you never know? Neither what good things are in store for you in the future, nor any bad things either: probably for the best isn't it, either way. I used to think in those days there was nothing for me at all in the future, that I hadn't a chance. I never thought of killing myself, I'm not the suicidal sort, but I couldn't see there was much chance of any sort of happiness.

Did I ever mention to you there was a second-hand furniture shop on the estate? I was having a hard struggle to make ends meet, so I used to go in there twice a week to look for bargains. Not for myself so much, more hoping I'd pick up something cheap and then perhaps sell it again for more than I'd paid. I couldn't buy much because I couldn't afford to, but as I got to know one or two people I let them know if they wanted anything I'd look out for it for them. I don't suppose I ever made more than a pound or two's profit a week because it was always small stuff; but it gave me something to think about besides my own worries and woes.

The man who ran the shop, George, was a really nice bloke: very unlike the sort of man I'd ever had much to do with before. He was very quiet and never had much to say for himself, and he was always polite and never a salesman. He never objected to me wandering round looking at his stock for hours. I think he had a pretty good idea what I was doing, buying the odd thing here and there and then selling it on again, but he didn't seem to mind. After a while he started to show me things he'd picked up cheap, and offer them to me at not much more than he'd paid for them himself.

He was a bit older than me but not much, and that was about all I knew about him. Another nice thing about him was he didn't ever ask me any prying sort of questions about myself. I never felt he was trying to chat me up either: he only talked about furniture. I forget what the actual item was now, but one day I bought something and asked him could he deliver it to my flat, so he brought it round on a Sunday morning with a friend: a wardrobe I think it was, or perhaps a chest of drawers. I offered them a cup of coffee and it was his friend who did all the talking while they were there; George sat very quiet and polite, but I think he could tell from the look of the place that I lived there on my own.

A lot of men would try to follow that up and take advantage of it, but not him. I went in his shop a time or two more, things went on as usual, and then one morning he invited me into his office at the back for a cup of coffee: he said he owed it me. Things after that still went on very very slowly: he was so shy, at times I'd almost the impression he'd never had anything to do with women in his life. It wasn't so, he'd been married and divorced but he certainly wasn't one for telling sob stories about what an unhappy life he'd had. The specially nice thing about him was just as he didn't push himself at me, he didn't ask me questions about myself either. I can truthfully say our relationship began as a friendship, and it stayed that way for six months at least before there was any question of anything more. It was me who made the running, and he was content to let it stay like that.

Eventually we did become more than friends, and he moved into my flat with me. The subject of marriage wasn't ever mentioned, and we never sat down and had heart-to-hearts about our pasts. I remember one day, which was the first time I'd ever mentioned it, I said to him 'You know I've been in prison, don't you?' All he did was just shrug. I felt I ought to tell him some more, so I said 'For a very long time.' His answer to that was only another shrug, and he said 'I expect that was all a long time ago.' When I finally did get round to telling him the whole story, it didn't seem to affect him in any way. He said something like 'Well that's all in the past now,' but no more. From time to time he told me a bit about his own previous life: he'd always been dead straight, his previous marriage had failed and he was happy doing what he did at his shop, selling second-hand furniture even if he wasn't making much more at it than just enough to live on.

The next thing after that was that I finally got a job as a telephone switchboard operator with a small firm of whole-sale newsagents and booksellers in the City. The job was advertised in the evening paper, and when I went along for the interview I told them straight out I'd been in prison for murder and I was only out on parole. I thought it would save time rather than me get the job and then lose it again with the help of the Probation Service. It was two elderly men in suits with glasses who interviewed me; but instead of falling off their chairs like I expected them to, they just nodded and said well if it was all right with the Probation Service, they'd take me on on trial.

I was really thrilled about it, and I worked hard: it was a chance and I was determined to make the best of it, never be late for work or take time off without telling them first or anything like that. The job didn't pay well and it was rather boring because it was such a small business and not very busy; but it was what I needed, a chance to settle down.

Then something else happened to me, and this was very important: I'd say it was the most important thing that ever happened to me in my life. Until that time I'd never been a religious person to any extent; and the way I explain that now, and which I firmly believe, is to say it hadn't been part of God's plan for me to be ready to experience faith until then. I hadn't ever been a big reader, but in this firm where I was working we did handle one or two paperback books about Christianity, and I started to get very interested in the subject. I do firmly believe God has a plan for everybody, and it's always working even though you mightn't know about it at any time. That was definitely proved to be so for me, because only a few weeks after I first started getting interested I was walking along the street on my way home after work, and a woman, a complete stranger, was just coming out of a church and we more or less banged into each other. She was about the same age as me and very friendly, and we started to chat. The finish of it was that she asked me why didn't I go along to the church the next Sunday, and see what I thought of it.

It's not a conventional church or what most people think of as one. We have a leader but not an ordained minister; anyone can give a prayer or say something about Jesus who wants to, and we have a lot of singing with that guitar group of young people. It's good fun, not solemn and sombre; and that's what I think religion ought to be. We've a congregation of as many as a hundred sometimes, white people and black people all together. It's totally changed my whole life. Some people would call it becoming a born-again Christian, but I don't think the name you give it is important. What matters is that you've opened your life to God and let him take control over it for you.

It had its comical side at the beginning though. George wasn't religious, in fact I don't think he'd ever set foot in a church in his life. He wouldn't go with me; but being the sort of person he is, he didn't try to talk me out of it, he left it to me to decide for myself. So it really shook him the day I told him we couldn't go on as we were, it was sinful to live together, and either we must separate or we must get married, and I wasn't going to sleep with him again until we were. I don't think he really thought I meant it at first. He said one marriage had been enough for him, we were perfectly happy like we were so why couldn't we just go on that way? I said no, I couldn't live with myself and God if we did, and he had to choose. He didn't argue: George never argued. He said if that was the way I wanted it, then that was the way it'd have to be. But he was too scared to ever again completely commit himself to someone for life, he'd been too badly hurt the time before to risk it. We didn't row about it: we had a long quiet talk, and we decided to part. The next morning was a Saturday and I went out shopping; when I got back he'd packed up his things and gone. He left me a lovely note on the table and some flowers, and that was it. When I came back from shopping and found them, I sat down at the table and howled. He was such a gentle spirit, and I thought I'd lost him.

He went to live with his sister, she had a flat near his shop, and altogether I think he was there about two months. I missed him terribly; but I examined my conscience, and I prayed to God to give me the strength to go on doing what I knew was right. I must admit I prayed to him once or twice too to bring George back to me if it was possible. And if ever I needed convincing of the strength of God's love for everybody, even someone who'd sinned as much as I had, I certainly eventually got it. One Sunday morning there was a ring at the flat doorbell, and there was George. He said he couldn't go on living without me and please would I marry him? Typically George, very short and straight and simple, just the one sentence. He said he knew I knew he didn't feel the same way about Christianity as I did, but if I'd take him with me when I went, he'd come to church with me now and then and see if it changed his mind.

It wasn't possible, for a whole lot of reasons that're all too complicated to explain, for us to have a church wedding: it had to be a registry office job. My church people were terrific about it, they were really happy for me that George had come back, and they made him so welcome he was really knocked out by it. I think one of the things he found most surprising was it gradually started to dawn on him that all the people in our church, young and old, they all knew all about my history and that I'd done a life sentence for murder. He asked me how they'd found out, and I said what was true, that they hadn't found out: I'd told them myself at a meeting one evening, when there'd been about thirty people there. He said that must have been a very brave thing to do; but I told him something else that was true, that it hadn't needed bravery at all, because I wanted to tell them and I knew long before I did they wouldn't turn their backs on me. I felt very safe and very loved among them, so it was easy.

I've been a Christian for two years; and then a year ago after he'd been to church a few times George said he wanted to start going regularly. Then before long, after that he said he wanted to be a Christian too, which made me wonderfully happy because I knew it'd bring him such happiness. Six months ago he became one, and we asked the church if we could have a ceremony of blessing on our marriage. Of course they said Yes, and last Saturday when we had it it was the happiest day I've ever experienced in my life.

What comes next, we'll have to wait and see what God wants for us. Even greater happiness, I'm sure of that. George is still working in his second-hand furniture shop, and I'm doing a bit of temporary clerical work now and again: the wholesale firm has closed down. We rent this nice little maisonette, we're involved in all sorts of things to do with the church like socials and charity fund-raising, or visiting people who are ill or in trouble, and trying to bring them the Lord's help and comfort. We'd both be happy to go on as we are.

I do have one idea though that's been in my mind for quite a while now. It's that most of all I'd like to try and do more for girls in prison or not long out of prison. I met more than enough of them while I was inside; I think we talked about it before, how they seemed to be dead set on going on wasting their lives after they got out again, with their heads full of crazy ideas still about glamorous lives of crime. Well I've been through all that myself, there's nothing they can tell me about outside prison or in it. I can tell them truthfully I was just like them, even a good deal worse than most of them. And I feel now if I could talk to them, be their friend, keep up a permanent support for them, that would be something really worth doing. I'd like to help run a hostel for them.

So I have the idea that before long I'm going to start making enquiries to see if the prison people'll even consider letting a lifer work with ex-prisoners. I feel every day more sure that this is what the Lord wants me to do. But if it doesn't work out, then I know that means he's got something else in mind for me instead. I'm happy to wait and see, very happy.

Oh heavens, hang on, excuse me, I must see to the oven, I can smell burning, I'd forgotten! I knew you were coming so I've baked a cake!

EIGHT

Big Bully Billy

WILLIAM DAVENPORT

A massive man in faded T-shirt and jeans, six foot four inches in height and weighing nearly twenty stone, he had to sit awkwardly sideways on the tiny two-seater sofa in the small front room of his terraced house. He talked in a quiet northern-accented voice, taking an occasional sip from a red and green striped glass tumbler of orange juice. He was thirty-two.

– When I was a lad at school, it was almost like I were royalty. Already by twelve or thirteen you know, I wasn't just the biggest boy in the class, I was the biggest boy in the whole school. It didn't bother me whether I was educated or not: the way I looked at it I didn't need to be, not with the status and reputation I had. I was big, heavy and powerful: I could knock anybody over just by giving them a shove. The whole school knew it and I did too, and I kept up my reputation by demonstrating it at least two times a week. I'd go up to one of the lads in the top class, anyone, it didn't matter who, just to pick a quarrel with him and provide the opportunity for having a fight with him. I kept a sort of mental list as to whose turn it was next, and if they'd not done nothing to me, I'd accuse them somebody had told me they'd said something nasty about me. 'Big Bully Billy', that was my title; and I did, I liked it. There was one day I remember when another lad's parent, his father, came up to the school to see the Head, to complain to him his boy'd said I'd been bullying him. The Head sent for me, and when I went in his study this bloke stood up, I think with a mind of telling me off. He wasn't all that small and he was quite well set; but on me he only came up to about here. So all he did was look at me and keep his mouth shut and sit down again. After he'd gone the Head said to me

'Davenport' he said, all reasonableness you know, 'Davenport, you don't want to get yourself the reputation of being
the school bully do you?' I said 'Oh no sir, no I don't,'
trying as hard as I could not to sound as though that was
exactly what I did want.

I didn't care a bit I wasn't popular. I think when you're at
school, the ones who matter are the ones one way or another
who stand out from the rest. You could be very clever, win
all the scholarships for going to university and that sort of
thing: well there was no hope of that for me, I was a right
thicko and never wanted to be nothing else. Or you was one
of the sporting ones, the best footballer in the school team,
the local Bobby Charlton; or if not that, you were an athlete
and could run and jump and win all the medals on sports
day. None of that was me either: I hadn't got the faintest
co-ordination of hand and eye, and when it came to running
or jumping I was just heavy and lumbering and made no
effort. Therefore all that left me to do was make a reputation at being the big strong lad no one would want to have a
quarrel with and everyone wanted to keep on the right side
of. It's not nothing to be proud of to say it now, but I used
to think it was: that a fair few members of the school staff
were a bit wary of me because of my size and reputation as
well.

There was no excuse for it; but I think if you come to
think of it, in one way I might have been a lot worse than I
was. What I mean by that is I didn't use my strength for
anything more serious than bullying. Whether it was
because the school I went to was in Rochdale, so not really
close enough to say Manchester or Liverpool for there to be
too much serious crime for a lad to get involved in, I don't
know. I think that might have something to do with it. But
perhaps it was more luck than anything, I never met the sort
of people who would have led me into it. I was never much
interested in crime, not thieving or nothing of that sort.
Another factor might be my family weren't criminal either,
they never had been and still aren't. My dad's an honest
hard-working man in light engineering, I've a brother who's

completely straight and my older sister's married with two kids. Neither of them so far as I know's ever done a thing wrong in their lives. And my mother's the sort of woman who'd go straight back to a shop if she thought they'd made a mistake and undercharged her, and my dad'd run around for change for a parking meter. About the only unsettling thing in my childhood was my brother and sister was both clever at school, and I wasn't up to their standard and I knew I never would be.

But things gradually dawned on me too, that I didn't need to have their education, I could do all right without it; not only all right, but better than they did in the way of earning myself a living. When they left school, my sister went into a bank and had a nice respectable job that earned her about enough money to go to the cinema once a week and have one week's holiday a year at Blackpool; while my brother, he was on into further education at a technical college, studying for certificates to get himself into electronics, so he never had no money either. But me, I was richer than both of them and my father and all, all added together, without any education.

From before I left school, the place'd always fascinated me was the local markets, specially what you might call the bits and pieces stalls: old clocks, lamps, china chamber pots, those old-fashioned silver cutlery sets in wooden boxes, I think they called them canteens – all those sort of things folk had thrown out because they didn't want to keep them no more. I used to spend hours and hours after school and at weekends, going round the markets and seeing what they'd got. And studying the prices: how much you could pick up tortoiseshell hairbrushes for at a stall in Oldham, how much you could sell them for to someone else who had a stall in Bury. By the time I actually did leave school, I'd already learned myself a really good grounding in prices and values, and I was well on the way to building up quite a nice little business in buying and selling. I never tied myself down to a stall of my own in one fixed place: instead I went to and fro all the time, picking up bargains and improving

my knowledge. It was all open and above board, I didn't
touch stolen stuff at knockdown prices with no questions
asked about where it'd come from, nothing like that. And I
didn't go in for pricey stuff either, that I'd have been out of
my depth with, like antiques.

I enjoyed the freedom of it, you know the fact I was
working for myself: I could decide what days and what
hours I was going to work, just as I liked. It was ironic
really. I'd no education, I couldn't add up and couldn't
hardly write my name; but it was at the time when those
cheap electronic calculators were starting to come in, and
for someone who was all the time having to consider dis-
counts and profits and all in percentages, they were invalu-
able. I'd no ambitions to become a big business man or
launch out on a big scale: I was happy making myself a
living, paying my mum and dad for my keep and a bit over,
and most of all I woke up every morning looking forward to
wherever I was going to bargain and buy and sell.

All I was was an ordinary lad, not very clever in the sense
of school education or things of that sort, but with a good
head for business work. That's how I'd sum myself up; and
as I started growing up and maturing a bit, I think I was
starting to be a nicer sort of a person too, in the sense I
stopped picking quarrels with people so much, and behaved
more responsibly and more grown-up like. I mean for
instance I never used my size to intimidate anybody in
business dealings, I never threatened or bullied any more. I
wanted to be liked, I wanted the people I did business with
to get to know me as someone who was friendly and reliable,
and always absolutely honest. By then I was eighteen, I
must have been one of the youngest market traders in
Lancashire, and I liked it that buyers and sellers who were
much older than me would deal with me like an equal.
Everyone always called me by my Christian name, and that
was something else I liked too. A lot of the middle-aged
women'd get quite motherly towards you, give you cups of
tea and cakes and stuff, ask you how your parents were: it
was all looking really good.

I've often thought it's funny how your whole life can be changed for ever, though, just like mine was, by one single chance happening. It's true, it can, and sometimes it is; but not very funny though sometimes, either.

– Where'd we got to last time? Oh aye, yes, I don't talk much these days, I'd sooner try and forget.

I had a lot of friends, young of my own age as well as older people I met on the markets, both male and female. I say friends but none of them was really close, so they'd be called acquaintances more correctly. I don't know if you know or not, but in the north of England particularly among the younger people, the great place everyone wants to get to is London. For a lot of youngsters it's not they specially want to live there, more just the idea London's got a sense of excitement about it, everything that happens happens there. For me, I was exactly like that; and up till the time I'm talking about, I'd never been there.

So this day, a Tuesday morning I think it was, I was on a car park in Bolton and I met this chap Keith, more or less my own age and doing the same kind of things for a living. We were standing by a saloon car, a big old Morris, and while we were chatting I happened to see the keys had been left in its ignition. I pointed to them to Keith, being a bit sarcastic like about people who did thoughtless things like that. Keith said, he was laughing and he meant it as a joke in the first place, he said 'I wonder if it's got enough petrol in it to take us to London?' And I said, it was still mostly meant jokingly, 'Why don't we see?' So we did, we got in it, Keith started it up and we drove out of the car park. We weren't car thieves, we weren't thieves of any kind, neither of us; to the extent we thought at all about what we were doing, we were going to do no more than drive around in it a bit, what they call joyriding.

That's not how it worked out though. Before long we were out of Bolton and heading in the direction of Manchester; and then we were continuing on from there,

Stockport, Hazel Grove, Buxton, still all the time laughing
about going to London if the petrol didn't run out. Derby,
Stafford I think, then Rugby; and by then it'd become
serious, we'd got far much further than we'd really
intended. In the end though the petrol did look as if it was
coming to a finish, so we drove into a transport caff and
parked it away from the main building, then we went inside
for a cup of tea. There was a lorry driver at the table who
asked us where we were making for: we were still being daft
and we said London. He offered us a lift so we took it, and
he dropped us off somewhere in north London, Barnet or
Enfield as far as I can remember. I know it was dark and we
were hungry and we'd neither of us any money, but we saw
a big hotel, a modern tower block sort of a place with a lot of
cars parked outside it, and decided we'd sleep in one of
them for the night. The next morning we were hungrier
than ever; but we saw a food van making a delivery to the
kitchens, and we hung about out of sight until we saw our
chance, then nipped in and stole a box of meat pies off it and
some milk.

Up till that point of it, it'd all been random and unplan-
ned, we'd no serious thought about any consequences.
What we intended was since we were so near London, we'd
go into the middle of it for the day, see some of the sights,
then hitch our way home back north again. We'd neither of
us any idea at all what a big place it was: to us where we
were on the north edge of it, Piccadilly and Buckingham
Palace and Tower Bridge and the rest, we thought they were
probably all about ten minutes' walk away. I suppose we did
see some of it, but the chief thing I remember is being tired
and hungry all day, and getting lifts in trucks and vans that
didn't seem to take us nowhere except another part of
London. Being country bumpkins we didn't know the
names of half the places or where they were in relation to
where we thought we were, and towards the end of the day
we ended up in a big sort of park somewhere towards the
south-west side, Ealing or round there. We were having a
cup of tea at a caravan tea bar near the entrance to the park

and we got talking with another chap from the north; he said he'd been living in London himself for four years, and he could take us to a working men's hostel where they'd give us cheap lodgings for the night. We fell on his neck.

It was a very peculiar place that hostel was. Some years afterwards there was a big scandal involving the chap running it, he was making himself a packet from claiming Social Security benefits for people who weren't living there, and it's been closed down now. But when we were there it was at the time when he was still thriving and hadn't been caught. He said he was full up, he didn't have any room to take us; but he said he had another place a few miles away, which was run for him by someone else he'd put in as a manager. We went there instead: it was pretty spartan and not very clean, with beds crammed in everywhere, not just in the bedrooms but in the corridors and basement as well. The so-called manager was a very foul-mouthed Cockney sort of a bloke, who we later found out had got a criminal record for violence of one sort and another. But as I say, we were very green: as far as we were concerned we were just glad to have somewhere to stay, specially when he told us he could get some payments through for us in a few days from the Social Security. He gave us some forms to sign, and I remember just as we were going to he said 'Don't do anything stupid like putting your real names.'

We stopped there about three or four days; no money arrived for us, so all we could do was hang around and wait. This Cockney bloke gave us a few pounds each for pocket money, and he said we could pay him back by doing errands for him. Like I've told you I wasn't very bright and I said yes, anything, I'd be glad to do it in return for him putting us up until our money came through.

The next day he said to me and another lad would we go in a little van he had over to the main hostel, and bring back a bloke there he wanted to talk to about a business matter. We thought nothing of it, at least I didn't: we went over to the other place, asked for this resident whose name we'd been given, and told him we'd come to take him across to our hostel. I didn't have any idea that this was a threat, and that it was my size that was being used to frighten him into coming quietly. He just nodded and said he'd come, and that he wouldn't give us no trouble; and me, I hadn't any notion why he should say that at all. We took him back to our hostel and left him in a room with the Cockney bloke. I didn't find out till a long time after that he knew where somebody was, and the Cockney wanted to frighten him into telling him. He succeeded, but as I say this was all going on with me knowing nothing about it and taking no interest. Thick as two short planks.

The night after, I was told there was another job for me, which was to go in a car, this time with two others, to somewhere else and bring another bloke over. The Cockney told me I was to sit in the back of the car with the bloke and I wasn't to let him out of my sight. I think he said he might give trouble, but by then I was acting tough and said he could leave him to me. I still didn't grasp the full meaning of it, what my purpose was and what I was getting into, which to put it bluntly was being a hired frightener. Anyhow, when we did get this bloke and he was put in the back of the car with me, by then it was beginning to dawn a little: he was a small middle-aged Irishman, and he was very nervous and kept asking me why Benny, who was the Cockney, wanted to see him.

Where we'd had to go for him was half-way across London; and after we'd been driving half an hour or more, he said he was bursting for a pee and could we stop for a minute somewhere? We pulled up in a space by the road where there was some trees, and this Irishman got out and stood with his back to us for a minute, as though he was peeing up against a tree. It was getting dark, and then suddenly the car driver shouted at me 'Catch him Billy!' because the Irishman was disappearing out of sight down a ditch he'd jumped into. I went after him, clumsy like always and lost my footing, and fell into the ditch on top of him; within thirty seconds the other two were piling on top of us in the ditch as well.

I'm not making excuses for myself. Everyone always says they don't remember don't they? It's true I don't: I can only say it was almost like a scrap in a school playground, all arms and legs and everyone hitting out in all directions. But there was a knife came out; it wasn't me produced it because I didn't have one, but whether it was the Irishman himself's or one of the others', I don't know. It kept getting dropped, and first one grabbed it and then another. But he was the one who got stabbed with it, and he was killed. He wasn't just killed, he was slaughtered: he had more than thirty stab wounds in him, they said at the trial.

We went back to the hostel, and we all just waited. I don't know if the others slept but I know I didn't: I just sat on the edge of my bed, I didn't eat or undress or anything. Next morning, very early just when it was getting light, there was a shout from someone upstairs: 'Police!' and I ran along a corridor in the basement, and I shoved up a window at the end and climbed out. There was a young policeman stand-ing waiting on the grass, just above my head. He said 'All right son, stay where you are and put your hands on top of your head, you're nicked.' He was about half my size, I could have picked him up with one hand; but I stood stock still like he said, and put my hands on my head.

– Prison, what's there to be said about nine years in prison that's greatly different from what anyone else can say? I was nineteen when I was sentenced, after I'd been nearly a year in custody on remand; my family were very good, even though I was in Brixton and they all lived up here in the north, they visited me regularly while we waited for the trial. I knew and they knew I was going to get life and there was no alternative to it; the only question would be how long I'd have to wait for the trial to come, and then after that how long I'd serve.

It's hard to try and describe my feelings when I finally did get sentenced: mostly relief I think, that the waiting was over. My parents were completely shattered by it, even though I'd told them not to hope for nothing different, but my own feelings were more like ones of resignation. I'd been responsible for the death of someone for no reason, who I'd no personal quarrel with, who I didn't know, who I'd had less conversation with than I've already had so far with you. What was a fair punishment for that? It's an unanswerable question: all you can say is whatever it was, it was less than I deserved.

The one thing I was determined about though, from very early on in my time, was I was going to try my best not to make imprisonment a totally negative experience. That sounds a contradictory thing to say: but I didn't come from a criminal background before it happened, and I wasn't going to let it turn me into a criminal after it. I don't mean by that that I'm not a criminal, because I am, of the very severest kind; but another lifer I got talking to not long after I started the sentence, I remember he said to me 'Try and do it with as much dignity as you can son: you never know, somehow some good might come out of it.' He was one of quite a few I met, older men doing longer sentences, who helped me. I tried to steer clear of the young villains and toughs, not get involved in the prison culture of fighting and drugs and homosexuality and trying to buck authority and not let them break me and all that rubbish. Instead I did as I was told, kept my head down and my nose clean, and kept plugging away at trying to find opportunities for improving myself. It worked too. I grew up, I matured: I went in a boy and I came out a man.

You hear of people in prison taking O levels and A levels and even Open University degrees. I knew from the start I didn't have the brains or intelligence for that sort of thing, but at least I thought I might get a bit further on from being nearly totally illiterate. I put in an application for full-time education: they gave me a few tests, and told me I was so far back I'd have to have remedial education, which is just to bring you up to a standard you can start from. To give you an idea, although I could just about read, if it came to writing something, I didn't know when the word for twice one should be spelled t-o, t-w-o, or t-o-o; or words like f-o-r and f-o-u-r, and t-h-e-r-e and t-h-e-i-r, I hadn't a clue about any of those either. I asked my mother to send me a dictionary in, and when I read something I kept looking up things and trying to memorize them.

In some prisons they've got a good educational system and in others it's quite a long way behind the times. I was very lucky to be in the ones I was in: Leicester to start with and then Nottingham. They had what they call that language laboratory system, where they give you a textbook and tapes to work with on your own, so you can go at your own pace, and don't get embarrassed by looking a fool in front of the rest of the class.

Another thing I did was wrote to my family and said would they tell anybody who asked about me that the thing I'd like best of all would be if they'd now and again send me a book to read. I didn't mind what kind of a book, any kind at all: westerns, thrillers, biographies, fiction, non-fiction, anything. I said tell them I was trying to educate myself, I'd only just learned to read, so anything and everything was wanted and the wider the choice the better. I had a fantastic response, my cell looked as though it had more books in it than the prison library sometimes.

If I had to chose the one that made the biggest impression on me of all, it was one I'd never even have heard of or known anything about if I'd not been in prison. It was sent in to me after I'd done about five years, by the sister of a friend of my mother's who's a nun. She sent it without writing a letter with it or anything: all it had was a card saying 'With good wishes'. It was a book of poems by T. S. Eliot, and it was called 'The Four Quartets': it's four separate long poems, and each of them's named after a small place somewhere or other, I don't know why but I suppose it's because that's where he had in mind when he was writing. The first one's Burnt Norton, and then the other three are East Coker, Dry Salvages which are some rocks off the north-east coast of America, and the last one's Little Gidding which I think's in Lincolnshire or Leicestershire.

When I first tried to read it, I couldn't make head nor tail of it; and I couldn't the second or even the twenty-second time either. But then suddenly one day it was like somebody'd switched a blinding light on, and it all started to have a lot of meaning and I could see what he was on about. I'd never read anything like it before in my whole life: it wasn't so much like he was talking to you as he was putting his own thoughts down on paper and letting you see them as they passed through his mind.

I read it and read it and read it, and there were great huge chunks of it I could say off by heart. Not because I ever sat down and learnt them because I didn't, but because they kept floating into my mind in the same way I imagine they did into his. I still remember how 'Burnt Norton' starts off:

> *Time present and time past*
> *Are both perhaps present in time future*
> *And time future contained in time past.*

and like I say, you have to read it twenty times before you understand what he's on about; but then once you do, you follow on his train of thought from there. Or another bit I always liked was out of 'Little Gidding' and it goes:

> *What we call the beginning is often the end*
> *And to make an end is to make a beginning.*
> *The end is where we start from.*

To me that sort of summed up my whole attitude for me when I came out of prison. I'd been lucky, they'd been fairly lenient with me and I'd only had to do nine years which was about average, and that was the end of that and I was going to start again from there. It's true to say without any argument at all that I came out better than I'd gone in: definitely as far as education was concerned, and with at least some improvement in personality too. It's very terrible it had to be at the cost of someone else's life though, that has to be said. It's something I can't undo, but it should never have happened; if they'd kept me in for good it wouldn't have been any more than I deserved, I'm well aware of that.

— At least I had my home and family to come back to, which is more than a lot of men who've been in prison can say. I had a good probation officer too: I still have her, and she's been a big help. I've been under her nearly five years now: three years since I was released, and before that she came several times to see me in prison and help me prepare myself for coming out. She told me it was going to be difficult to find work and she was right; but she suggested while I was working out from the prison hostel I should use some of the money I saved up to take myself driving lessons, which'd give me a qualification that might come in useful.

I passed my test the week after I came out. Then I started looking for work. I don't know how many jobs I went for but didn't get, and I got very depressed about it. One of the things I told my probation officer I'd decided was I was going to come out with the truth about where I'd been and what I'd done right at the beginning of every interview I went for. I began to think that was what was stopping anyone employing me: I still don't know whether it was or not, there's no way you can be certain. Sheila, that's my probation officer, she began to wonder about it too, I know: but it'd been my idea and not hers, and I wanted to stick to it as long as I could. Because she could see not working was getting me down, she fixed me up doing voluntary work driving goods about in a van for the WRVS; and that did help me having not so much time to sit around thinking about what a hard time I was having. I'm not a drinker so I didn't have much social life, and I didn't see how I was going to make friends except round the markets, which was something I didn't really want to go back to again, I'd lost the interest.

But they say if you're patient and wait long enough something'll turn up, and in my case it did, or rather two good things did. I started going to church a bit, and I found at our local one they had quite a big social group of people round about my own age, in their early thirties. A lot of them were young married couples, but I was lucky enough to meet there the young lady Marian who's now my wife. She was a very quiet shy sort of person, and it took me a heck of a time to pluck up courage to ask her out. She knew all there was to know about me, because I'd told the group my story soon after I joined, in the same way I told people I was asking for jobs from. None of them turned their backs on me, but I thought a young single woman might not be prepared to go as far as going out on her own to the cinema or a disco with someone who'd done what I'd done. There weren't any worries there though, she treated me quite normal as though I was any ordinary person, and she always has done.

She was one bright spot that stopped me getting too down: like Sheila she always went on encouraging me to keep on trying for work. The other one was that after a while, the driving around in the van I was doing for the WRVS made me start thinking: there seemed to be an endless number of people who wanted parcels or small items taken from here to there, so I asked round local small firms and businesses to see if they'd find the same kind of thing useful. Most of them said they would, so I decided I'd try it as a business. And I thought well if you don't ask you'll never get; so I went to the bank and told them about the idea, and said would they give me a loan to buy a van? I was surprised they said yes, they'd loan me two thousand pounds: which they did, and I bought a nice looking second-hand van and got started.

It was a struggle at first, but it's what I'm still doing, and I've not looked back from that day on. I work very hard, sometimes eleven hours a day even on Saturdays or Sundays, but I've built up some very good connections, and I cover here and the surrounding area over something like about two hundred square miles. People know I'm always on call and I'll always deliver within twenty-four hours, and I've got some jobs on contract now, which means I've got a sound regular work base.

Two years ago Marian and me got married, then last year when we found she was pregnant we started house-hunting and found this place, which is near to both her parents and mine. It was the very cheapest we could find: it's two up and two down, with the bathroom and lavatory built on as an extension at the back. We bought it seven months ago just before our Anthony was born. We were both over the moon when the building society said they'd give us a mortgage: I was self-employed and didn't fancy my chances would be too good and I could only offer a very small deposit. There it was though, they did. I was very lucky, and that's like I've been in a lot of ways in my life, there's no one more conscious of that than me.

Now I've been out four years, Sheila says the time's coming up when she wants to apply to the Home Office for lifting the conditions from my licence. To tell you frankly about it, and this is no reflection on her, I don't think in my case it's going to make any difference to me one way or the other. It doesn't matter whether I still have to go on reporting to her or not, as far as I'm concerned. She was a great help to me in the beginning, gave me a lot of support; but the things that've made all the difference to me have been first the education I got in prison, second having a home and a good family to come back to, third getting a job and building it up to where it looks like it's going to go on, and fourth and most important of the lot is having my own family. Marian and Anthony are everything to me, and we hope there'll come a time when we've got sufficient money to afford a brother or a sister for him.

Our life's very ordinary and simple: for me it's mostly work with a few hours off when I can find time to take them, and for Marian it's looking after Anthony and me and the house. It might not seem a very interesting life to anyone else but it's something I never thought in prison I'd have a chance of ever again. And I still say what I said the other night: I can't justify to myself or anyone else that there's any way I really deserve it.

NINE

Something terrible has happened

PHILIP DERBYSHIRE

– It was nine o'clock on a Sunday morning. I went out to go and find my wife. I knew I had to find her and tell her. I went to her mother's first, I thought she might have stopped the night there but she hadn't. Then I went to her sister's and she wasn't there either, so I started going round her friends. I think it was at about the third one that I found her, at a girl's she knew called Pat. I said to Pat 'Can I speak to Lorna please, will you please go and ask her to come to the door?' When she came I asked her to come home with me, but she wouldn't at first, because of the big row we'd had the night before. I said 'Please Lorna, please you must come home with me, something terrible has happened.' She must have been able to tell from my face it was serious, because she nodded and said all right then she would, only I'd have to wait while she got some clothes on.

There was hardly anyone about in the streets at that time on a Sunday morning, everywhere was very quiet. We neither of us said a word to each other. We walked back to the council flat where we lived, and I opened the door. Our three-year-old, Lucy, was standing in the hall crying, so Lorna picked her up and cuddled her and told her it was all right, she was back. I asked Lorna would she please go into Jack's room and have a look at him, she said why what was the matter? I said 'Give Lucy to me would you, please go in and have a look at him and see if he's all right. I think I've done something to him, I think I've hurt him very badly, please go and have a look.'

She went down to the room at the end of the hall and unbolted the door because I'd fastened it so Lucy couldn't get in, and she went in. After a minute she came back, she didn't look at me, she just stood and looked at the wall. She said very quietly, 'You've killed him Phil. He's dead.'

I knew it. There was nothing to say. I gave Lucy a little kiss on her cheek, and said to her 'I'm very sorry love, I don't think I'm going to see you and Mummy now for a long time.'

– It has to be said. I want to say it to you first so you can make your mind up. He'd been crying all night and when I picked him up out of his cot at six o'clock in the morning he was still crying, he'd made the bed sopping wet and he'd dirtied himself all over. I shook him and I hit him to stop him crying. He went on. He'd never liked me and he was doing it deliberately, so I punched him some more and swore at him. I kept shouting at him and hitting him. I was shouting 'I know you don't like me you little bastard. Tell me you love me. Go on, tell me, tell me.' There was still a fire alight in the grate from the night before and I threw him in the fire. He still went on crying, so I picked him up out of the fire and I put him in the sink and poured boiling water over him from a pan. Then I hit him and punched him some more, and swung him against the wall. I don't know the exact point he stopped crying at, I don't know exactly when he became dead.

I put him back in his dropside cot and I sat down for a long while with my head in my hands, thinking at what I'd done, which was battered my eighteen-month-old son to death and caused him to cease to exist. Then I heard Lucy wake up and start crying in the other room, so I shut the door and bolted it after me and went in to her. I said 'Now you be a good girl and stay here and don't go in the other room because I've bolted the door.'

It has to be told first, you have to know about it so you can decide whether you want to come and talk to someone like me, a person who did what I did.

Sometimes while he was speaking he lapsed into a long silence, looking down bleakly at an unlit cigarette between his thumb and forefinger, his lighter held forgotten in his other hand.

Sometimes as he stumbled through recollection, his eyes looked like caverns of horror, still incredulous with disbelief at what had happened, though it had happened more than twenty years before.

He was living alone in a large furnished bed-sitting room, and was out of work. He ate little, and subsisted mainly, he said once with a short laugh, on cigarettes, beer, coffee, nice girls, sandwiches and tranquillizers. Dark haired, stocky, with a trim beard.

– Lorna and me got married when we were both eighteen. She was pregnant, but that wasn't the reason for us getting married, at least not on my part and I don't think on hers either. She was the girl next door, and I'd been in love with her since I was fourteen, all my teenage years she'd been the only girl for me. We were both in the same class at school in Derby, and we used to go to school and come home together pretty near every day.

I was a bit of a rowdy and a bit of a show-off, and I was in trouble from a fairly early age: stealing bikes and motor bikes and motor cars, and a few other things too, if it was somewhere me and my mates could break into easily like a tool warehouse or a copper tubing store. They say if you get into crime as a youngster it's because you come from a broken home or you mix with bad company, but that wasn't true in my case. My mother and father were happy and still are, my brothers and sisters have all been straight all their lives; and as for mixing with bad company, I'd say I was the bad company that other lads got in with, I was always a bit of a leader that way. Lorna could have been a steadying influence, but it wasn't her fault she wasn't, she didn't like me thieving and being in trouble.

When I left school at sixteen I had a whole lot of different jobs, but none of them very satisfactory. Chiefly it was because I wasn't too interested in the idea of working for a living. I was quite good at mechanical things and I'd work for a few weeks in a workshop or a garage, but then after a few more weeks I'd not bother to get up in the morning, and decide I was going to look round for some thieving to do instead.

The first time I got sent away was to detention centre for three months, for taking and driving away a motor car, driving with no licence and insurance and the rest of it. We were living with Lorna's mother, and I got my sentence on the same day she went into hospital to have Lucy. Detention centre's not much good at doing what it's supposed to, which is deter young men from a life of crime by subjecting them to the short sharp shock idea. In my experience, for myself and what I've seen it do to other people, it usually has the opposite effect. It gives you a status, you can't call yourself a proper villain unless you've done at least one DC.

Selfish, thinking of myself naturally all the time. I knew Lorna would be all right at her mother's and when she brought our new baby up to show me, I made the usual promises about how when I came out I'd settle down and get a steady job, but it was no more really than talk, I think we both knew that. I can look back from my middle forties like I am now and say I was very immature and Lorna was very immature, both of us nothing like grown-up enough to have a baby and start a family. But you could say that of a lot of young people, thousands and thousands, and somehow most of them get by.

Anyhow, despite all the promises which I think Lorna had the sense not to believe too deeply anyway, when I came out life went on in more or less the same way, at least for me it did. A bit of work, a bit of villainy, a bit of work again, like that. About all that was different was because of having the baby we moved up to the top of the council waiting list and we got a flat. We thought that was great, but it wasn't long before the other side began to show up as well. Lorna had a baby to look after and it took up a lot of her time, the baby didn't sleep well and it got her down, and she missed living at home with her mother. She started getting very depressed. The way I'd put it is to say she was picking at me and nagging me all the time about not having a job and taking risks over stealing. She had a point about it, she was more right than I was, but I didn't admit it. We had some big quarrels and shouting matches, and she walked out on me more than once and took Lucy with her back to her mother's. However much we quarrelled though, it was true when I said she was the only girl I ever loved, it always ended with us getting together again.

Another thing I can say with hindsight about the way we weren't mature, is that when we had a quarrel we never sat down and talked things over like grown-ups, we sparked each other off into shouting and fighting. I've got better at doing that now and I think she has, but at the time when we needed to we didn't have the ability to do it.

It wasn't long after we got the flat that Lorna fell pregnant again, and around then was a time when I did start to worry a bit. Only my way of worrying was to put more effort into villainy, not into working. The result was I got into more trouble and ended up by getting sent to borstal. So there was Lorna on her own again, with one small baby and another one on the way, and her husband in borstal. I still don't know what it was first put it into my mind that she'd conceived when I'd first gone into custody on remand before getting the borstal. But when she came to see me, that was what I accused her of, and told her I knew the baby she was going to have wasn't mine. I was definitely trying to hurt her, and I can only think I was doing it because of my own position. You hear a lot inside about men there whose wives have babies that aren't theirs, it's natural that it happens. But I'd no real reason for accusing Lorna at all, and I knew I hadn't. I do think though that whether I really believed it or not, that's when I first began feeling resentful towards Jack and letting it build up in my mind. He was born while I was in borstal, he was with Lorna and I wasn't, he was coming between us: I think those were the feelings I had. I had these swings of mood while I was inside, that I was going to disclaim him and have nothing to do with him because he wasn't mine. By the time I came out it'd really got very strong inside me, I was very mixed up about what I felt for him. By that time he'd be fourteen months old I suppose.

We'd had a very hard time with Lucy when she was little, because she cried a lot and gave us a lot of sleepless nights. I'd thought Jack might be better but he wasn't, he was worse. Lorna and I used to have these big rows about whose turn it was to get up and see to him and change him, and I really didn't like doing it: I thought it was the woman's place to do all that. On top of that I felt Lorna loved him more than she loved me; and I was sure he loved her more than he did me, I thought I could tell from the way he looked at me he didn't like me. I'd not started being part of his life until I came out of borstal and by then he was fourteen months, so in every way I don't know what I expected from him at that age, I was someone who was a complete stranger to him. I put all these thoughts and intentions into his head. I know it was wrong of me, I knew it was wrong of me then, but that didn't stop me doing it.

On the night before I caused his life to come to an end, Lorna and me had had another of our big quarrels and she'd walked out saying she was going back to her mother's and she didn't care about me or the kids. She was pregnant again then, but I didn't know that. Lucy was old enough to know what was going on, and I remember when I put her to bed she put her arms round my neck and kissed me, and she said 'It's all right Daddy, I'll look after you until Mummy comes back.' She and I always had a close relationship. I just dumped Jack in his dropside cot in the other room and switched the light out and left him. I don't think I even fed him, and I know I didn't change him: it always disgusted me when he was wet and dirty.

He yelled and screamed all night, and I didn't sleep, I just lay there feeling hatred for him.

At my trial on my counsel's advice I didn't give evidence. I think he thought whatever I said would only make things sound worse, so I admitted everything and stayed silent. Counsel said he'd nothing to offer in mitigation, and in his summing-up the Judge said I'd been examined by doctors and psychiatrists, and they all said there was no sign of mental illness or abnormality. He gave me life which was what I expected.

Sometimes before talking he'd stand at the window, staring out at nothing, as though waiting for an inner thought to come, to help him begin.

– Words are funny things you know aren't they? I think about the last thing I said to you last time was the Judge gave me life. But that's not describing it really, because when I went to prison I was totally emotionally dead. I didn't feel anything, I didn't want to feel anything. I didn't want to think and I didn't want to know what anybody else was thinking or feeling about me either, I couldn't face the prospect of it. I stayed that way in prison for more than four years: when my parents wrote I didn't answer their letters, and when Lorna wrote after a while and said she'd had another baby girl and'd like to bring her to show me I didn't reply. I didn't want to be in the present, I can only put it like that. But I didn't want to be in the future either, I didn't want to think about living in it, everything was pointless, even thinking about it being pointless was pointless. It wasn't sorrow or self-pity, I don't recollect doing much crying or feeling sorry for myself. It was a sort of total numbness, a sort of being in a complete state of shock if you can be in a state of shock for as long a time as that. When someone was talking to me the sound of their voice would suddenly switch off and go very faint, like they'd moved into another room and I could hear them talking through the wall. Or sometimes when I was saying something, I'd stop what I was saying in the middle of a sentence and turn round and walk away. I'd been put in prison, and then in there I'd put myself in another prison, locked myself away so that nobody could see me or get at me. Nobody's ever said it to me, but the person I wanted least of all to see me or get at me was obviously me myself.

I'm still often very much in that same frame of mind now, I have been for the whole ten years since I came out. I'm very frightened of emotions: other people's but particularly my own, I won't uncage them or unchain them, not ever again. I've been holding them in for so long I don't think I could now even if I wanted to. I don't want to though and I don't think I ever will.

After four years inside I began to unfreeze a bit, in a way, on the surface you could call it. They say that's about the average length of time it takes for most people. No, it wasn't anything special happened to do it, only that I started to realize I had to face up to one day perhaps being released and living outside again. It's not waking up, it's not a birth of hope or anything soft and sentimental like that. In some people it takes the form of religion, or a girl starting to write to them. For me it was a long bloody agonizing fight against reality: I wanted to stay imprisoned, not to have to think or feel, and struggled as hard as I could not to have to face it. But it was no good, the knowledge was there inside me all the time that I'd done what I'd done, and however much I wanted to stay sheltered from the consequences, I couldn't stay sheltered for good, I'd have to face people.

I wrote to Lorna and said if she still wanted to come and see me, I'd see her. It was a long time before she replied, but in the end she did, and I sent her a visiting order and she came. It was over five years since I'd seen her, but she'd hardly changed. Nor had my feelings for her either, I still loved her deeply. I told her I wanted us to get a divorce. She said she didn't want that, however long it was going to be before I came out she wanted us to try again. I said no I didn't want to. She said she still loved me very much, but I didn't say the same in return, only going on saying that I wanted to be divorced. Then she told me that two years after I'd gone inside she'd been going to have another baby by another man, but she didn't want anyone else's babies but mine and she'd had an abortion. She and the chap involved had been intending to get married but it'd broken up. She said but despite that, if I'd still have her she'd like to stay married to me and she promised to wait for me. My only reply was it made no difference one way or the other as far as the abortion and the other man were involved. They didn't come into it; and nothing to do with that, but I still wanted a divorce. She cried, she wrote me a long letter afterwards asking to think it over some more. But I wrote back the same thing, that I wouldn't change my mind.

I was frightened. I was frightened just because I loved her, that all my emotions would break out again. I wasn't going to let that happen again, not ever. In the end she agreed and we got divorced. It's a hard thing to explain to someone, a hard thing to explain to myself, that because I knew I still loved her I had to get divorced.

I don't feel much like talking tonight, shall we go and have a drink?

Other nights he started to talk immediately, almost compulsively.

— I was thinking tonight before you came, I was saying to you last week wasn't I, or the week before, about emotional immaturity? It's a strange thing. I don't know why, but I think I did sort of choke up inside me when it happened, and I've stayed more or less at that emotional age of around nineteen or twenty ever since. It's struck me because since I've been out I've had a whole series of girlfriends, and nearly every one of them's been a girl of that age, eighteen or nineteen. It's still going on while I'm well over forty: the girl I'm living with at the moment is eighteen and the one before her was and the one before nineteen.

No, I don't think of women, perhaps I should say girls rather, just as objects to screw. I definitely don't like one-night stands. I'm not one for them. It has to be a proper relationship, a love affair. That's not the same as being in love, well it isn't for me; I always say to the girl at the beginning it's not going to be permanent, it'll only last till one or the other of us wants to move on. No strings. I don't always keep to it though, I get jealous. But it has got to be a sort of semi-permanent arrangement, at least for a time, going steady together, living with each other, not in and out of bed a couple of times and then that's it. I'm always straight about myself, about my record and what I've done: and I can honestly say I've never had an affair with a woman yet who it's made any difference to. I don't know exactly how many there've been altogether, ten or twelve in total in ten years perhaps. But there's not one has ever left me because of that reason. Most times it's been me who's brought it to an end rather than them, my attraction to them starts to fade.

It's hard to say why. Now I come to think about it – I think this is true but I've not thought all that deeply about it before – as soon as any suspicion starts coming into my mind my feelings are in danger of going to start getting too deep about someone, then that's the end of it, I want it finished. I like sex, I like making love, but what I can't cope with is any kind of mental intimacy. I don't know how to deal with emotion, not real true emotion, I'm frightened it might run away with me. I have to keep love affairs on a very superficial level: a laugh and a joke, playing around, never talking about anything serious or deep. I don't think I could have a proper full grown-up relationship with a woman because I wouldn't let it get anywhere near starting. This may be something I'll grow out of. I don't think so though. The only woman still that I love really is Lorna and I'll never go back with her.

Yes, sometimes I do talk about it with her, yes. The last time she and I talked about it was only last year. She doesn't live far away, we've always kept in touch; sometimes if we run into each other in town we have a cup of coffee together or something. She wrote to me and said could we meet specially, she wanted to have another talk. I knew what it would be about: the same thing as it's been before, couldn't we have another try? She's never married again, and both the girls have grown up now and are married themselves.

This time she said she'd talked to them about it, and they both agreed it'd be nice if we married. I said no like I always do, and she must have told them that I'd said it. Within a week they both wrote me letters saying how much Lorna wanted it and asking me to think again.

I daren't though, I just daren't; I'll never be able to explain that properly to her, or the girls, or to you or anybody else, least of all to myself. I know it'd be wrong though, I do even if I can't say why. I said to you once I didn't believe in God and I don't, not really. But there might possibly be a supreme being of some kind. I feel I'd be tempting fate or whatever you like to call it, and something terrible would happen again, there'd be some kind of revenge. There's been too much that happened for there ever to be forgiveness. An innocent child died at my hands, it's not something can ever be wiped away.

Yes, yes that's correct. If there ever was to be forgiveness for me, given by a god or by Lorna as I think she has done, or my daughters, no right it'll still never be given me by myself. If every single person in the world, in this one and the next, if they all said Phil we forgive you, I'd still never say it to myself. The world is lacking a person because of me. That thought's always there in my mind at the back, and sometimes it comes sweeping forward to the front and blots out everything else. I'll be sitting in a café, or in a bar of a pub, or even just walking down the street, and I'll see someone who's a young lad of about twenty: and I find myself looking at him and, and I can't take my eyes off him because the thought like explodes in my head. That that's the same age Jack would be now, he might look just like that young man, talk and stand and move in exactly the same way. And Jack isn't going to because of me.

More than once I've thought if we'd still had the death penalty and that's what the Judge had passed on me as a sentence and I'd been hanged, that've been the end of it. Sometimes I've thought that could never have been as bad as sentencing me to go on living with all this remorse. They don't let you out you know, it's one of the things they take into account before they do, until they're sure you show contrition for what you've done. Jesus I've felt it and I go on feeling it. I've had treatment of all sorts, inside prison and out, for depression, paranoia, suicide feelings, but none of them has ever cured me. The most that's ever happened has been the symptoms have been alleviated: a little and only for a little while, and then they come back. There is no cure, not for me. The end of my life, that'll be the cure. Nothing else.

I have to face it's not just me dwelling on it either. It's always on the record, it's always there in other people's minds too. About three months back I went up to London for a couple of days and while I was there I rang Lucy up and said could I go and see her, I'd like to see how she was and where she lived, and their first baby they'd had not long before. She said yes of course I could, her husband had had to be up in Scotland on business, but she'd cook me a nice meal with a bottle of wine. Which she did, and we had a lovely evening and a really good long chat. She showed off her baby to me and he was beautiful.

When I came back I told my probation officer all about it and how good it had been. I told her how nice Lucy'd been to me, how lovely her baby was, how I'd played with him on a blanket on the floor when she'd slipped out to the shop on the corner for another bottle of wine and some cigarettes. My probation officer keeps me under close supervision, and writes reports every couple of months about where I've been and what I've been doing. So I always tell her everything, not just for that but because she's interested. I knew she'd put it all in, but nothing crossed my mind or hers either about it to be truthful I think.

What came back was a letter from the Home Office. Pauline, that's my probation officer, she didn't say anything when I went in to report to her, she just handed it to me to read. It said she was to tell me in the clearest possible terms I was never to do such a thing again. I was never ever to allow a situation to arise, on pain of being put back in prison if I did, when I was on my own with a small baby. That was

what they were telling me, more than twenty years afterwards about myself and my own grandson. When I read it I
felt I had a mouthful of ashes in my mouth.

– You decide this week what you want us to talk about. No
yes anything you like.

Yes right, the only way is to be quite frank about it. The
reason why after ten years I'm still under such supervision is
I've a bad record. Pauline'll tell you if you ask her. I've had
a couple of very near misses, when I could easily have been
recalled. Daft things, stupid things Tony. I drive motor cars
when I've had too much: I'm banned from driving and have
had my licence taken off me, but I still go on doing it. And I
get in fights and get charged with assault. I haven't got at all
a good record under supervision. Last year I hit a bloke who
was flirting with my girlfriend at the time. He took me to
court. I got a big fine and a stiff letter from the Home
Office, a really stiff one. Irresponsible is the only word you
can use for my behaviour.

Why? Well . . . well you see I think one of the troubles
has to be that deep down inside me, I don't really care if I'm
recalled to prison. Being inside has got no fears for me, in
my mind I'm a prisoner whether I'm inside or out. Every
time I get in trouble and the police are going to take me to
court, the probation officer looks at me and she sighs, and
she says 'Well I'll come and speak for you Phil, but how
long it'll go on that I can keep you outside, I really don't
know.' I haven't the heart to say to her 'Look Pauline, give
up, it doesn't matter if they recall me, honestly it doesn't.'
She comes to court and goes on making excuses for me.
Perhaps not excuses, that's not the word, but she says I've
got big problems and I'm trying my best, and putting me
back inside's going to be no help. Then she takes me back to
her office and gives me the biggest bollocking you'd ever
hear. She's having her own private war with the Home
Office on my behalf and she's a terrific person to do it, but I
feel bad about letting her go on doing it.

Her supervision? Well it varies in its closeness. Sometimes she'll let me see her only once a month; then if she
feels I'm going through a bad patch emotionally, she'll
make me see her once a fortnight, or even once a week. In
the last two years she's kept me on a pretty tight rein. I
resent it, oh yes I do, often. But she's always straight with
me. Every time she sends in a report on me, she shows me
what she's written and says I must write on it too, put my
own comments at the end. We have big rows, I flare up and
complain, but she always stays cool and controlled. She's
very clever you know. I've never met a woman like her, I've
never met a person like her.

Pauline talks to me sometimes about me having some
form of psychiatric help. Only although I talk about it with
her, I never get so far as actually agreeing to her making
enquiries to get it for me. I tell her and it's true, I find it
very hard to talk. A couple of years back a probation officer
in the area started a group of lifers, we all met in his office
and talked about our problems facing up to a life after life.
There were four of us including a woman, one time they
were five. What it seemed to me was we were such completely different individuals we hadn't really got any common problems at all. The woman had killed her husband
because he knocked her about and though she regretted
killing him, she wasn't really sorry he was dead. One of the
men had killed another man in a brawl in a pub, and I don't
think he was too much troubled by it. To him it'd been a
straight fight which he could have been the one who got
killed himself in. The other person I forgot what they'd
done.

But you see what I remember most was that even in a
group like that, I felt I was a total outcast. I was someone
who'd done something far worse than the rest of them.
There was always a detached part of me looking at it from
outside that said that was true, I wasn't like they were in any
way. Their problems were of coming to terms with being in
prison a long time, then having to take up the threads and
try to get back into ordinary life. Mine weren't: they still

aren't. Mine are a different kind, to do with the crime itself, which whatever way you look at it was violent, inhuman cruelty, perpetrated on a defenceless child. Strong words, yes, very, but not strong enough. We talked about it once a few weeks ago didn't we? You asking appalling questions, me giving appalling replies? But your words, my words, none of them cover the true extent of the appallingness of what I did. You ask, I reply. We both listen to my replies and twenty years after it happened I still can't believe it, that the person I'm talking about who did those things to his own child was me.

Yes you could be right to say that, yes. I do feel prison's where I belong. There are good days and bad days, but even on the good days that feeling doesn't change. The immediate surroundings don't affect it one way or another. I read a book by a lifer once, I think he called himself Zeno after a Greek philosopher who had a stoical attitude to life. He said the same, he belonged in prison. I'm no philosopher myself, I'm not even sure what a stoic is. It's nothing to be proud of and nothing to be brave about, just a dull ache and a knowledge that if the truth's to be said, I'm beyond the pale of ordinary society and couldn't ever get back inside it again. I don't think I'm properly living in society and never could because I'm not a fit member of it, I only belong to it in theory, I'd put it like that. I'm outside humanity, both in humanity's eyes and in mine.

– I'll tell you something. Nobody else knows it and I don't know why I should tell you, but as it's our last night I will. In that top drawer of that chest of drawers there, under my socks and handkerchiefs and things, buried at the bottom underneath the piece of newspaper lining the drawer, there's a little packet. It's a brown envelope fastened up with sealing tape. If ever there was a fire and I had to run out of here, that's the thing I'd go for, to grab to take with me. Even if it meant leaving every other thing in the room behind I'd take that. Wherever I've gone, it's always gone with me, I carry it to every place I go to live in. But I've never opened it and looked inside it, not once and I'm sure I never will. I asked Lorna for what's in it when I came out of prison, and that's how she gave it me, fastened up in an envelope. It's a photograph of me and Jack she took in the park a couple of weeks before I ended his life.

TEN

My story

BETTY DREW

At the age of sixty, Betty Drew has now been out of prison on licence for nearly five years. She can claim to be the longest-serving woman life-sentence prisoner ever: she has done thirty years.

She lives in a ground-floor flat in a council-owned house in north London, a few hundred yards away from a large municipal park, which has formal gardens, woods and wide open spacious heathland. In the distance across it in cold weather when she's throwing sticks for her dog, she looks like a small rubber ball. Exactly five feet high, she wears an old navy blue duffel coat, baggy brown trousers, thick rubber knee-high workmen's boots, and a voluminous waterproof cape. Wound round and round her neck is a thick dark green woollen scarf, and on her head a black felt cap with a little peak and earflaps. Her apparel makes her girth almost the same as her height.

Her grey hair is cropped short with a fringe. When she talks her voice is loud and brusque: she waves her arms, puffs incessantly at cigarettes, and stabs them out half smoked one after another in an overflowing tin ashtray in her lap. She sits upright on a large old armchair with her legs sticking out in front of her because they're too short to reach the floor; and under them back against the chair lies her huge black and brown Alsatian, its head between its paws and its baleful eyes wide open and staring, looking instantly ready to leap forward at the slightest movement it might not care for.

Talking with her was as difficult as trying to interview a fully turned-on bathtap. Words poured out of her in an endless tumultuous flood, and could never be stemmed or even momentarily checked by questions or interventions of any kind, however blunt. She talked on over every interruption, following her train of thought further and further away from its origin until she'd

*totally lost sight of it: but continued talking with increasing
fervour as each new thought brought to mind the random next.
(One but only one example of this is given as an illustration in the
text.)*

Before long I began to despair of finding a method of bringing
shape or coherence to what she said, and became depressed and
exasperated. She meantime became increasingly enthusiastic, her
confidence and expansiveness growing daily. After all her lonely
and unwelcoming years, she at last had someone to listen to her. I
began to dread the increasing nearness of a point when I would
have to say, however rejecting and painful it would be to her, that
I couldn't continue. After almost a fortnight all I had was an
amoeba of sound which daily split up and reproduced and
multiplied itself to double its size in each conversation we had.

I misjudged her: when I finally conveyed the difficulty,
fragmentarily but insistently between her downpours of reminisc-
ence, she suddenly said she could see the point. But she would like
to go on, she said, if there was any way of doing anything about it.
As a result we drew up a list of the principal periods of her life,
and she talked about them, and only about them, from notes she
prepared each time in advance under different headings. She
decided which were the important ones she wanted to speak about
herself, and which others were 'unimportant so you can fill them in
how you like'.

That solved one of the difficulties, but another remained
unresolved throughout. I am terrified of Alsatians.

Age 20	Convicted and sentenced for murder.
Age 27	Released on licence.
Age 28	Recalled to prison after seven months to continue serving sentence.
Age 32	Released from prison after being kept in for a further three years.
Age 33	After six months, recalled to prison to continue serving sentence.
Age 46	Released after being in prison for a further thirteen years.

| Age 48 | Having been out for nineteen months, recalled to prison to continue serving sentence. |
| Age 55 | Released after serving a further seven years' imprisonment. |

– My story. Part One. My childhood. I was born in Barnstaple and I have one sister younger than me by two years. My mother never wanted me, she beat me and shut me in cupboards and things like that. I was a noisy little girl and I was once told I'd been difficult since I was two. My father was on the railways and he adored my sister Sally, he loved her much more than he loved me. He died when he was forty-seven and I was thirteen, and I've always felt guilty about it all my life because it was when we'd had a quarrel. He was angry with me about something and I shouted at him, and he had a heart attack and died before the doctor arrived. You can't ever say you're sorry afterwards, and I would have liked to because I did have warmth and affection from him sometimes. I would sit on his knee and he would read to me, stories but also information books like encyclopaedias. He used to send up for sets of books from newspapers. Some of the ones I remember are the *Complete Works of Charles Dickens* in twelve volumes, the *Harmsworth Encyclopaedia* and the *Complete Works of Shakespeare.*

I was much closer to my father than I was to my mother, she didn't like me because I don't think I fulfilled the idea of what she thought a girl should be like. My main impression of her is she wasn't a person who gave out affection, and I don't know whether this is true or not. When I've thought about it since I've thought she probably didn't have a very happy life either. She didn't talk or laugh much or play games with me and my sister like my father did. She was an aloof person. For instance she never told me anything about sex. When I had my first period when I was about twelve, I found blood between my legs and I was very frightened and I ran into the kitchen to tell her. She didn't say anything at all, she just said with a grim look 'Stay there' and went out of the room. When she came back she put a packet of sanitary towels on the table and she said 'There you are, from now on you'll have to use these once a month.'

Another time I was asking her questions about marriage and why did people get married and what was it like? She didn't answer the questions properly, all I remember her saying was that when a girl grew up she got married, and that then meant her husband had certain rights. She didn't say any more than that, so I asked her what did it mean, what were the rights, and she just said she wasn't going to talk about it and I'd find out for myself.

I can't think of anything else about my childhood, except to say that on the whole it wasn't either happy or unhappy, mostly just normal.

— Part Two. My life as a young girl, being in the sanatorium and how I met Janet. Up to and including killing her.

I didn't have much education, I spent a lot of time off school because I wasn't a healthy child, when I was fifteen I was diagnosed as having tuberculosis. In those days they didn't have all the drugs for it that they do nowadays, it was very serious for you if you'd got it, and a lot of people died from it. You had to go into a special hospital called a sanatorium where there were a lot of other people who all had the same thing. The only treatment there was was that you had to lie still and rest all the time. You were coughing and spitting blood and so were all the other patients and a lot of them died. It was very frightening to be a young girl in a place like that. The only thing everybody always talked about was dying. It was an enclosed world, and you didn't feel anyone else understood you except the other patients. They'd got the same illness and they were the only ones you could talk to, not people from outside at all. It was a bit like prison, nobody who hadn't experienced it really knew what it was like.

They had education classes there but they weren't very good and I missed out on a lot of things. Either you felt too ill to go to the lessons, or often they couldn't get teachers because they were frightened of coming into contact with people who'd got tuberculosis. So that did make it a very enclosed world like I've said.

You formed very intense friendships with other people because you had this threat hanging over you all the time, that you were suddenly going to get worse and die. Sometimes they'd let you go home for a weekend but that wasn't very successful. You felt your family were holding you at arm's length in case they caught it too, and people didn't come to see you for the same reason. I never minded going back to the sanatorium, I preferred that to being at home.

My special friend among the other patients was Janet who was a girl who was two or three years older than me and very pretty. We used to go for long walks together in the sanatorium grounds, and sometimes we held hands and a few times we kissed each other. We were both very innocent and there was nothing more in our relationship than a very big affection for each other. We read the same books and played gramophone records and danced together in the recreation room. I had a big crush on her and she had a crush but a smaller one on me. In those days there was a lot less frankness about such subjects than there is now, and you didn't talk about such things as lesbianism because hardly anybody'd ever heard the word or knew what it meant. Nobody even thought of ever doing anything physical together. So I should describe what we had as a close lesbian relationship but without sex.

From time to time you could be discharged from the sanatorium for a trial period and go home and see how you were. Janet was married and her husband sometimes came to see her but they weren't very happy together and she said she didn't like living with him but she'd nowhere else to go. She said he didn't like living with her either because he was frightened he was going to get TB. Sometimes she was at home when I was in the sanatorium and she came to visit me. The other way round, when she was in there I'd visit her. And of course sometimes we were in there together. It went on in this way for between two and three years, and then it came to one day when I was out and she was coming out, and I asked her would she like to come and live at our house. I'd spoken to my mother and sister about it, and they were agreeable and we had a spare room.

We were both having what they call a long remission of the illness and we used to talk about what we'd do to start a new life together in the future when we were both completely better. But we also quarrelled a lot and this was chiefly my fault because I was very jealous. She was a very quiet person but I was very noisy and aggressive and used to physically attack her. Then I'd burst into tears and say I was sorry, and she always put her arms round me and we made it up. From time to time she would go to see her husband for a day or two and I was always miserable and unhappy when she did, and worried in case one day she didn't come back.

Then one time she told me she'd been and he'd demanded his rights and she'd had to give them to him. This was the same phrase my mother had used that time I told you about. I didn't know what it meant so I asked Janet, and when she told me it made me feel sick. I didn't want her to go, but I told her it was disgusting and she must leave the house. She packed her bag and said she was going to her mother's, and she left.

I was in a state of fury, and I told my mother and my sister I was going to her mother's house to kill her. They tried to prevent me but I went, and I took with me a hunting knife with a deer-horn handle that I'd bought the year before. I really intended it for if I ever met her husband. I went to Janet's mother's house and her mother opened the front door, and then Janet came out and we stood on the front path and I was shouting and screaming at her. Her mother tried to drag Janet away but I lunged after her and stabbed her in the chest with the knife. I stabbed her just the once but very hard, and they say it went right through the breastbone just about here.

At that moment my mother and sister arrived in a taxi

because they had been worrying about what might happen. Then the police came as well and they took me to the police station and charged me with attempted murder. This was because at that stage Janet was not yet dead but she was dying.

While she was in hospital before she died she made a death-bed statement saying what had happened, and that I'd threatened to kill her before, which was true. Then she died so the charge became murder, which in those days was a capital crime, that is one you could be hung for because there was still the death penalty.

While I was in prison awaiting trial I became seriously ill again with tuberculosis and had to be kept in the prison hospital. A QC came to see me and he said he'd do his best for me but he didn't give much for my chances, the police had got a lot of love letters I'd written to Janet and they were going to read them all out in court. A doctor came and examined me and he said he didn't think I was going to live very long anyway. I felt very ill in the hospital wing of the prison but I didn't feel they treated me very kindly. I'd murdered somebody, I'd written the sort of letter that one woman wasn't supposed to write to another one, and I'd got TB, so everyone treated me as though I'd got three things they didn't want to come too close to, and they kept their distance.

By the time it came for me to go to court I was coughing up a lot of blood. They told me I was to lie very still all the time, and when I said I was going to plead guilty they said that was good because it meant I wouldn't have to be cross questioned and move about, and they could take me into court on a stretcher. Which was what they did and they got two packing cases to lay it across in the well of the court.

SENTENCE OF DEATH ON 'DYING' GIRL
Sentence of death was passed yesterday at Devon Assizes by Mr Justice Pilcher on twenty-year-old Elizabeth Anne Drew for the murder of twenty-six-year-old Mrs Janet Margaret Jones of Plymouth. The jury, who included three women,

took seventy minutes to reach their verdict. Drew, who was said to be suffering from a severe illness which was probably incurable, heard the verdict apparently without emotion from the stretcher she was lying on in court, and was afterwards taken by ambulance to the County Gaol.

Prosecuting Counsel said that Drew fatally stabbed Mrs Jones with a dagger because she refused to return to live with her and that this was a premeditated act. He said, 'It was clearly a case of cold-blooded callous murder.'

Principal Prison Medical Officer Dr R. Brown said that while she was in custody on remand, Drew had refused to be interviewed by him. But he had studied all the evidence and documents carefully, he said, and in his opinion the accused was sane 'when she drove the dagger into the dead woman's body'. He did not agree when questioned by Drew's counsel that she did not know what she was doing. He agreed that he had no qualifications in mental disease except experience.

Defending, Mr J. C. Maude, QC, submitted that Drew had a disease of the mind and at the moment of the murder did not know the difference between right and wrong. He also referred to her serious physical condition, and said it was not possible to estimate what effect long treatment including the administration of drugs could have had on her. He asked the jury to return a verdict of guilty but insane.

In his summing-up to the jury, Mr Justice Pilcher said the jury had only one short point to consider. 'She is guilty of murder unless you think that at the time of striking the blow she was insane within the meaning of the law.' He said it was quite clear that during their association, Drew and Mrs Jones had formed a perverted passion. The jury might feel disgust or sorrow that that sort of thing should exist, but no doubt the prisoner was 'passionately attached' to Mrs Jones. 'The state of her mind is a question of fact, and therefore is a question for you, members of the jury.'

(From a contemporary newspaper report.)

– What the Judge said to me when he sentenced me to death. I didn't need to write it down because I can remember it exactly word for word off by heart. He said: 'Elizabeth Anne Drew, you are twenty years of age and it is my duty to pass upon you the only sentence which the law can pass for the crime of wilful murder. The sentence of the Court upon you is that you be taken from this place to a lawful prison, and thence to a place of execution, and there you suffer death by hanging, and that your body be buried within the precincts of the prison in which you shall have been last confined before your execution; and may the Lord have mercy upon your soul. Take her down.'

– My story of what it was like the first time I was in prison.

After I'd been sentenced to death I was taken to the condemned cell in Exeter prison. The first thing they do is weigh you and make up a bag of the same weight as you are, and practise with it on the end of a rope so they can work out what the right length of drop for you should be. If it's too short it won't break your neck, you'll just hang there and slowly strangle to death, and if it's too long you fall too far and it can jerk your head off. The condemned cell is next to the execution shed with just a door in between so you have only to walk a few steps when they come to hang you, and you can hear them practising with the bag at night when they think you're asleep.

My mother and sister came to see me every day but there was always glass between us, and they were always embarrassed and couldn't think of what to say. I didn't really want to see them anyway. The other person who came every day was the prison chaplain. I told him not to because there was nothing to talk about, but he went on coming and kept asking me had I changed my mind about repenting.

Altogether I was eight days in the condemned cell and doctors kept coming to examine me. I felt as though I was dying from my illness and the amount of blood I kept coughing up, and I hoped I'd die before they came to hang me. Then one afternoon the Prison Governor came into my cell with a letter in his hand which he said he had to read out to me. It was from the Home Secretary and it said in view of my health my sentence had been commuted to one of imprisonment for life. After he'd gone the prison officers in

my cell all shook my hand and congratulated me. I thought
it wasn't very sincere of them because from the looks on
their faces they seemed to be thinking I was so ill I was
going to die anyway, and they were relieved I was saving
them the trouble.

The day afterwards I was moved to Holloway prison
where they had a proper hospital. A Scottish doctor came to
see me and examined me, and he told me he was determined
to save my life. I didn't like him, and I told him I didn't
want to live, but he said he was going to do it whether I
wanted it or not. He sent me to an outside hospital in
Middlesex for an operation for the removal of one of my
lungs. I was there for ten days and then I was sent back to
the hospital wing at Holloway and I spent nearly two years
there under treatment from this doctor. He said I needed
rest and care and not to work. He was a very strange sort of
man, very Scottish and very abrupt, and in all the time I
knew him he never once smiled or gave me a kind word.
Everything he said was very gruff: 'Turn over so I can listen
to your back, cough, put your clothes back on,' all the time
like that.

Then one day he said he'd done all he could for me and I
was as good in health as I'd ever be, but I was to look after
myself and if I ever felt tired I was to go and lie down. He
told all this to the prison staff too and said I was only to do
light work, so they put me in the library. As I gradually got
my strength back I became very aggressive again and was
always arguing and fighting and getting into trouble. Stop it
Elsa. The Governor called me into her office one day and
said they couldn't do any more for me at Holloway, they
were going to send me to Askham Grange where it would be
up to me and how I behaved how long it was before I was let
out on licence.

I didn't like Askham Grange any better than Holloway
and I still kept getting into trouble up there. Elsa's getting
restless because it's past her feeding time and she wants me
to feed her and take her out for her walk, so I'll have to stop
in a minute. In the end at Askham Grange they told me they

were going to let me out on licence. I'd been in prison altogether I think it was between seven and eight years. All right Elsa shut up, now stop barking, I'm going to feed you in a minute. At Askham no she's not going to are you my beauty no you're not, all right then we'll have to stop and go on from there tomorrow.

– My story of what it was like the first time I came out of prison. This was a very long time ago, nearly thirty years ago and I get confused sometimes between things that happened the first time I came out of prison and things that happened other times that I came out.

The first time I came out I went to live with my sister Sally who was living up in Glasgow, where she'd gone when she got married a year before. I didn't get on with her, but if you could give an address where you were going to live when you came out it helped your chances of getting released. We started to quarrel as soon as I got there, and after only about a month her husband told me he wasn't happy about me being there so I left.

When you've been in prison about the only people you've had a chance to meet were other prisoners, and quite a few of them when I'd been in Holloway had said if I was ever short of somewhere to live while I was looking for somewhere else I could always go to them. You're not supposed to do that, the authorities won't let you give another ex-prisoner's as an address, but I'd given my sister's place so I knew they wouldn't know, and I went down to London. I stayed with several of the girls for a few days each, and knocked about round the West End which was somewhere I'd heard of when I was inside but never seen. It wasn't long before I started taking drugs, but I didn't do prostituting like a lot of them did. Drugs were expensive though, and you had to do things like thieving and shoplifting to get money for them.

It was awkward for me to stay anywhere for long in London because I wasn't reporting to the probation, and I

knew if the police picked me up they'd put me straight
back in prison again. After a few weeks I went back to the
West Country to my mother and said could I go and live at
home back with her. She wasn't very keen on this but I
said I'd get a job and work and pay towards the house. To
prove I was turning over a new leaf I went and reported to
the probation there, and told them I was sorry for moving
from Glasgow but I had to because of my sister's
husband. I didn't say about being in London in between.
They said so long as I behaved myself it would be OK. I
started a job as a market gardener but only stayed there a
week because I had a row with another girl working there.
She knew of my case from reading about it in the local
papers years before when it happened, and she told the
owner of the market garden I was a lesbian murderess and
she was frightened of me and didn't like working with
me, and he said I had to leave. I had one or two other jobs
after that, shop assistant and things, but I was always very
quarrelsome and getting into arguments with people and
threatening to hit them.

I've got a note here which starts: Had something died
inside me being all that time in prison? I think the answer
to that's Yes, I'd been all that time in the sanatorium and
then in prison. I was unsettled and my mother and me
were not getting on, so I went to Bristol where there was a
girl living who I'd been in Askham Grange with.

She had a flat and her boyfriend had moved out, and
she said there was room for me to stay there for a while
which I did. I got a job in a factory kitchen. One day there
was a letter from my mother to say the police had been
round making enquiries and where had I gone, but she
hadn't told them. She said they'd told her they'd had a
complaint from a woman in the town who I'd worked for
for a few days until I quarrelled with her. She said I'd
been making obscene telephone calls and threats to her.
The police told my mother if she knew where I was she
was to tell me I was in big trouble because I wasn't
keeping the terms of my licence, not reporting to my

probation officer, changing my address without notifying, not working and all the threats I'd been making people as well.

The girl I was staying with in Bristol, she was always bringing men back to her flat and we had big rows over it. I got fed up and left and I went back to my mother's. I was only there two days and the police were on the doorstep again. They said the girl I'd been stopping with in Bristol had told them I threatened to kill her, and when I'd gone she'd found all her clothes in her wardrobe had been slashed with scissors. They told me I was going to be taken back to prison on what's known as recall to prison for not obeying the licence terms. You don't have a trial or anything, you're kept in prison until the Home Office have been notified, and then they decide whether you should serve some more of your life sentence or not. This was what they decided in my case I should, and it was three years before they let me out again.

– The second time I came out of prison. The second time I came out of prison was after I'd been recalled for three years, all of which time I spent in Holloway. That was a period when drugs first started coming into prisons and they were brought in on visits by visitors. I never had any visitors but there were so many drugs about that other prisoners would get them for you. Therefore when I came out I would say I was by then what would be classified as a drug addict.

At one time it looked as though they weren't going to be able to let me out, because neither my mother nor my sister would agree to me going to live with them. If you don't have an address to go to you can't go out, so I had to wait until one of the women's hostels run by the Salvation Army would give me a place. I stopped there for a few days and then I got a job as a petrol pump attendant on a garage forecourt, and moved out of the hostel into a furnished room of my own in Paddington. I had a probation officer who was very strict with me, he made me report to him twice a week. When I said it was awkward for me because I was working, he said that was my problem and if I couldn't do both, both work and see him, then seeing him came first and I should find another job.

I put up with that for a couple of weeks, and then on the spur of the moment one day after I'd been paid instead of going to report to the probation officer I went to Paddington station and caught a train to the West Country and went to see my mother. She said I could only stop there one night and in the morning I must go somewhere else, she didn't mind where. I'd not got out of bed the next morning when the police arrived in a car and took me all the way back to London to the probation officer's office. He said I hadn't had his permission to go and that meant I was in breach of my licence and he was going to have me put straight back in prison unless I gave him my solemn promise that I'd never do it again.

I gave him my solemn promise but it didn't mean anything, because by then I was so dependent on drugs I wasn't really in the real world at all. I was in a very bad state. I was so bad I even went back to Holloway prison and asked could I see the Governor. I told her about my problem and how bad it was and she said if I'd go back and see her again two days later, she'd try to find a place for me in a clinic for treatment. When I went back she said there was a clinic and they would take me, but only if there was a proper referral to them by probation. The Governor said it wasn't in her power to refer me because now I was out I was officially the probation people's responsibility not hers. She said would I give her my permission to tell the Probation Service I was badly dependent on drugs, and I said no I wouldn't because after the way they'd treated me I thought the Probation Service were a load of – well I won't say what the expression was I used, but I told her there was no way I was going to tell them I was a drug addict. She asked me to think about it very hard and said she'd even come with me to the Probation if I wanted her to but I wouldn't agree.

It wasn't difficult to get drugs in London. There were

certain known doctors who all the drug addicts knew who would give you prescriptions, and there were people who made a living out of stealing prescription pads and printing their own headings on them with those kids' printing sets you can buy, and you could write your own. I knew one girl who said getting drugs was easier than getting aspirin tablets, she could get anything anyone wanted any time and she didn't do it for the money, it was a sort of philosophy to her. The man she lived with played his guitar in the Underground, I think it was at Bond Street Station on the Central Line, he was a chap who'd had a university education but he didn't agree with the establishment world, he said children should be free. Another of his ideas was that people shouldn't have to go to school when they were kids, they should only go when they wanted to and if they didn't want education until they were grown up it ought to be OK for them to choose the time themselves. Then he and this girl broke up, they had a lovely little girl who they called by the name of 'Free' which I always thought was a lovely name. I don't know what happened to him, but she went out to Africa to teach black children and then someone told me some years back she'd come back to England and gone all religious after going to hear Billy Graham preach, so then she'd gone to America, California or somewhere where it's always nice and sunny and you can pick oranges off the trees, great big ones as big as that, as many as you want and it doesn't cost anything for them at all. I'm not very fond of oranges or any fruit really except I like an apple now and again. Elsa likes apples too, don't you darling, she likes a piece of apple if I'm eating one. That's very unusual you know, you don't often hear of dogs liking fruit do you? Most dogs are carnivores and only eat meat and I've often thought I'd like to be vegetarian myself because it's much more healthy for you and perhaps if people didn't eat so much meat there wouldn't be wars and things because it's bound to affect you eating blood isn't it, I'm not saying I believe in vampires and silly things like that but I remember there was a film with was it Peter Cushing in it once and every time he even

so much as smelled blood his eyes went all glazed over.
Another actor who used to be in those horror movies was
Basil Rathbone, but my favourite actor of all time was Fred
Astaire, oh he was such a lovely dancer, him and Ginger
Rogers they don't have films like that at all nowadays or at
least they don't seem to.

What? Drugs, oh yes, well I always had my pockets
crammed full of drugs in case I couldn't get enough sup-
plies. I didn't deal in them, well not unless I was very short
of money sometimes, mostly I exchanged them one for
another and tried them all. One day I had a fight in the
street with another woman who had drugs, and the police
arrested us. Because I was a lifer I was taken to court and
recalled to prison again for not reporting and possessing a
large quantity of drugs.

*After this second recall, she remained in prison for a further
thirteen years before being released again.*

*That it was such an inordinate length of time was due to
several factors, of which the first was her bad behaviour
throughout the whole of the time she was back in custody. She
was violently aggressive towards both members of staff and other
prisoners, and was frequently involved in fights. Punishment
had no effect on her: she was kept for long periods in solitary
confinement, lost pay and privileges, and was moved round
several different prisons to see if any change of scene or regime
could bring about any improvement in her behaviour. None did.*

*On three different occasions during the thirteen years, it was
felt she had made some progress towards the point when another
release date in the not-too-distant future could be considered as a
possibility. Three times she was moved out of a closed prison and
into a hostel inside its walls, from which she went out daily
without supervision to work, returning again in the evening by
the specified hour, usually six o'clock. This transitional period of
testing before final release usually lasts, for most prisoners serving life sentences, between four and six months.*

*Three times she broke the hostel regulations, either by fighting
with other inmates, bringing in drugs or, on one occasion,*

returning drunk late at night in a taxi. Each time she was taken off the hostel and put back inside the prison again, and had to wait another two or three years before she was once more considered for possible future release and given a further trial period of outside working.

Eventually, at the fourth attempt, she survived long enough on the hostel without getting into trouble to be released on licence once more.

— My story of what happened when I came out of prison for the third time.

Well I felt very lost and not knowing what to do, I think when you've been in prison all that length of time you can't help feeling like that. I was getting on to being nearly fifty and I hadn't had any training in anything so I couldn't do much for a job. Also I found it hard to get into the habit of work and living on my own, when you have to get yourself up in the morning. In prison every day of your life the officers come around shouting it's time for everyone to get up and you get used to that, to getting up and going for your breakfast at the time you're told, going for your dinner at the time you're told, going to work at the time you're told and your tea, and going to bed afterwards when you're told. And your work is there, only across the other side of the yard, you don't need to catch a bus. And it's always there, you can't get the sack from it. It isn't like that on the outside, you've got to do everything for yourself.

I had a room that the probation people got for me, it was in south London and I had a lot of different probation officers. I think no one wanted to take me on because I had the reputation of being difficult and aggressive. I worked at different jobs only I never stayed long at any of them because I had an argumentative nature. I didn't have any friends because I didn't really know anyone. In one of the houses I had a furnished room in, in Peckham, there was another woman, she was very big with great big arms and shoulders like this. I think she'd been in prison herself but I didn't know her. One night we had a fight when she came and knocked on my door, she said I'd pinched something out of her room which I hadn't, and I went for her with a knife and tried to stab her. The police were called and I was taken to the police station where I was charged with attempted GBH, that's grievous bodily harm. When the case came to court the following week the woman had disappeared so there was no evidence against me and the charge was dropped. I think the woman had a record herself and was wanted for something, which was why she ran away.

The probation officer told me I was lucky because if the case had been heard I'd certainly have been recalled to prison again, but it wouldn't have worried me if I had. The probation officer told me he didn't think London was good for me, because even though by that time I was off drugs permanently there was too much trouble I could get into there. He advised me to go back to the West Country and see if I could find my mother and try to make it up with her. I didn't want to do that, but I thought he was right about London, so this time I went to Exeter and then to Plymouth.

I was put under a probation officer there who said he was going to supervise me very closely and he was going to straighten my life out for me. I don't know what he meant by that because he never did anything except make me see him once a week. He asked me how I was getting on and I said All right and he said good, come back and see him again the following week, that's all. Oh yes and he said I should try and get outdoor work, I was better working outside where I didn't feel so hemmed in. I got a job for a while in one of the public parks pushing a wheelbarrow about, and another time I went to a quarry and asked them if they'd give me a labouring job, but they wouldn't because I was a woman.

Things went on much the same, most times I was out of work and lived in lodgings on what I got from the unemployment money. The landlady at one place reported me to the probation officer for being aggressive and troublesome and always quarrelling with the other people there. He persuaded her to let me stay on, but in only about two weeks I think, I had another quarrel with her and her daughter, and I went to my room and got a knife which I threatened them both with.

I was taken back to court for breach of licence again. You're not supposed to possess knives or anything that could be classed as a weapon if you're on licence, so I was recalled to prison again. The probation officer came to court, and he said on my behalf that when I'd been released at different times before, the longest I'd stayed out then was six months and this time it'd been eighteen months which was progress of a sort. It didn't really make much difference though, I was put back inside.

In deciding whether or not to recall a life sentence licensee to prison, the authorities' first consideration is not the punishing of the offender, but the risk to the public if he or she is allowed to remain at liberty. The nature of the offence committed in breach of licence is therefore of prime importance: and here was Betty Drew at the age of fifty threatening two people with a knife, thirty years after she'd stabbed and killed someone else. In addition only a few months earlier, although the charge couldn't be proceeded with, she had narrowly escaped prosecution for the very serious offence of grievous bodily harm.

She remained back in prison on this occasion for another seven years – for the same period of time, in fact, that she spent there after she was first convicted. Now sixty-one, she was released again four years ago, and since then she has so far remained out of trouble.

– Like you said, this week for our last talk I've made notes about things I'd like to have said more about, or things that haven't been mentioned that I'd like to have had the chance to talk about. They're not in any order. You said jot them down as they occurred to me so that's what I've done.

Number one, education. I didn't have much of it because of the sanatorium and prison, but I did get an O-level English language, or what was the equivalent of one, not that it has ever been of much use. I would have liked to have had more education, and when I was in prison I wish I'd been taught a skill of some kind that would have helped me get a job when I came out.

Number two. The number two thing I've written down is that I'd like to have said more about my father. All my life I've felt that my sister was my father's favourite. I didn't understand emotions at all, I felt like it's shown in films, that there are only two kinds of people, good people and bad people, and you love the good people and hate the bad people. I couldn't understand you could have the two feelings both together for one person. This caused a lot of conflict in my mind about my father, which is still there even at the age I am now. Another thing I think is I lost the wrong parent when he died, I was only thirteen and I think I'd have done better if he'd stayed alive and my mother had died. I was very upset about him and I felt guilty because of the feelings of hate I'd had for him. He died right after our quarrel and I think in a way I was responsible for him dying. Also my father was a strong person physically and mentally, and afterwards I judged all men by him, to me he was the ultimate of what men should be and I never met anyone who came up to it. I think that's why I turned away from them.

Number three, am I a lesbian? This is the question you asked me one day but I never properly answered it. Nobody's asked me directly like that before, and I didn't know what to say. I've thought about it a lot of times since, and I think the answer is No I'm not a lesbian, at least not in the way that most people mean it. I don't like men but then I don't like a lot of women either. I've never had a proper sexual relationship with anyone. In prison you can't avoid a bit of sexual contact now and again, but I never went looking for it. There was one instance some years ago but I'll not say which prison it was in because the other person was an officer. We did talk about how we liked each other and she was married and not long before I was due to be released she left the Prison Service so she could find a place for us to live together when I came out. I was working out from the pre-release hostel at the time and I used to meet her for a cup of tea. The week before I was due to finally come out I rang her up to fix our usual meeting and she told me she wasn't going to meet me because it was all over and she didn't want us to ever meet again. She didn't give any reason for it. Instead of going back to the prison hostel on time I went in a pub and got drunk and didn't go back until eleven o'clock at night in a taxi. My punishment for that was to be taken off the hostel and put back in the prison and have my release date taken off of me.

Number four, Elsa my gorgeous dog. When I came out last time the probation officer who came to see me to talk about my release arrangements and who was going to supervise me, the third or fourth time she came she had her Alsatian dog with her, or bitch rather, that she'd brought with her. She was the most beautiful dog I'd ever seen, and when I looked at her I said to Linda 'That dog's pregnant.' Linda said 'Yes she is, her puppies'll be ready just about the time you come out, would you like to have one?' So that was how I got her. Linda found this flat for me from the council, and the day I moved in she was eight weeks old and she brought her for me. She is the reason why I've stayed out of prison because she's my only friend, she's my companion and support. I take her for two long walks in the park every day, rain or shine, winter or summer, and I never get involved in anything with anybody, and I try not to talk to anybody too. Because if I ever got in trouble again I'd have to go back to prison, and then who'd look after Elsa? So I couldn't do that, not to my Elsa I couldn't possibly, could I my darling? You're the most beautiful creature in the world aren't you, you're the only true friend I've ever had.

Next note, my probation officer Linda. She is a very good person, she's much younger than me, I suppose only about thirty-eight, and the only probation officer in my life I've ever had any time for. She's very straight with me, she tells me exactly what she thinks, and if I swear and shout at her which I do when I lose my temper, she swears and shouts right back at me and uses the same swear-words I use. I tell her all about my life and my problems, and she tells me about her life and her problems, and it's like having a good friend.

Hang on, I've another note here which says Elsa as well, why've I got two? It says 'Tell about Elsa and Linda', well I've just told all that haven't I? No wait a minute, I remember what it is now. It's about Elsa and Linda as well and I didn't know which one to put it under. Yes. Right. One day when Linda went to a party at one of her friends' houses, she met a man there who is an Area Sales Manager or something for Pedigree Chum dog food, and she told him about me and Elsa. She said she thought Elsa was the reason why I didn't get in trouble any more and have stayed out of prison as long as I have done this time. She didn't tell me why, but she asked me could she give this man my address so long as it was completely confidential. I said yes she could, and a week later I got delivered to my door here a three-month supply of Pedigree Chum dog food and the same of mixer biscuits, and a note saying I was going to get this every quarter. They've never missed once, it's always on the dot and it's been going on like clockwork for three years. It's a huge saving for me in expense. No one has ever contacted me from the dog food firm or asked me for anything in return.

I've got another note here, it's only short. It says 'I was a lifer and I didn't know where to live except prison, prison was my home.' That's not very important.

This is something else I jotted down, I think it was Tuesday morning when I got up. 'I'm very embittered by humans and I like dogs better. Dogs understand you, humans don't. Dogs don't threaten to leave you and they don't tell you to get out and leave them. They take you for good or bad.'

Another note is this one. 'All the time through my life

I've always felt completely fucked up in my mind. I've never known really what was real or what wasn't, whether it was people or feelings that mattered.'

This is another. 'Prison officers try to destroy your individuality so they can manage you in a mass better, and they often nearly succeed in doing it. Then when you come out your probation officer tries to build up your individuality so you can act like a person again. I think it would be a good idea if they got together and decided which it was they wanted to be done with you.'

This one says 'I have always been a failure with all human relationships. My mother didn't want me, my father died, my sister and I didn't get on, I killed the woman I loved, the prison officer who I had a sort of love affair with gave me up. The closest relationship I've ever had is with my dog.' That's you my beautiful isn't it, yes.

This one is number, well it doesn't say. I stopped putting numbers on them. It says 'The recall I feel bitterest about is the one where I hadn't done anything, which I think was the second one. I hadn't done anything except have drugs. I was put back in prison because it was the easiest thing for the authorities to think of to do with me. I was very difficult to the Probation Service, and if you're difficult they have you shut away. When you're convicted you get a first-class solicitor and barrister to defend you but after that you're on your own. On a recall you aren't allowed to have anyone to defend you, you're found guilty and put straight back for as long as they like. Not because you've done anything all that terrible but because they think you might do something and it'd be a risk.'

This is the last one, I wrote it this morning for you because you were coming. I've written at the top 'Tell Tony' and it says 'I think I've proved I can stay out. I'm getting on to being an old woman now, and I think I've toned down a lot. I've never known what was wrong with me and I've never had a nice home like this, and I've never had a beautiful dog to feed and take out. What makes the difference is having some person or animal who's dependent on you for their life like Elsa is on me. We're dependent on each other and that's what makes the difference.'

ELEVEN

The theory of deterrence

ALAN ROBINSON

– I'm a living example of what they call the theory of deterrence mate. Listen to my story, and don't do what I did. I killed a policeman, and if you do that, you're dead. Because they're never going to stop hunting you until they catch you: no way, not ever, are they going to stop. You can murder an old lady, or a child even, and you might get away with it for a while; who knows, in some cases, you might get away with it for good. Now and again people do, right? Praps because they can't find you, or maybe it's not even known you done it. But not if it's a policeman you've killed mate, oh dearie me no, no most definitely not. If you've killed one of theirs, they're going to put all other crimes to one side, if necessary take every policeman off of traffic duty and let the whole of society grind to a halt. The number one priority over everything else in the world is catching you: and they're going to be devoting theirselves to it twenty-four hours a day, day and night. Or twenty-five hours a day, thirty, thirty-six, a hundred hours a day, or just so ever long it takes. They're going to catch you, they're going to convict you, they're going to throw you in gaol, and then they're going to leave you there for ever and let you stay there until you rot. Did I say I was a living example of deterrence? Well wrong word mate, I'm a dying one.

Alan Robinson killed a policeman when he was nineteen: a young policeman the same age as himself, also nineteen. Passing the mandatory sentence of life imprisonment, the Judge commented that the case was 'a terrible and a sad one, not of one wasted life but of two, for obviously this young man will now be spending most of his life in prison'. Up to now it has been eleven

*years: last year he was told he could not expect to be
considered for parole for another nine years.*

*A large flabby man with dark hair and brown eyes,
wearing prison overalls and a coarse open-necked flannelette
shirt, he sat at the table in the small unused store room,
talking in a deep voice and clasping and unclasping his big
hands to check their trembling. From away down the corridor
outside, occasional shouts and banging of doors: the sounds of
the routine day of prisoners and warders, rowdy and pointless.*

— You'll have to forgive me mate, I'm nervous see. I've
not had a visitor from outside since two years last
November, you get you forget how to talk to people in
ordinary conversation, know what I mean? In these places
it's a question of if you've got something to say, shout it,
cos otherwise no one'll hear you, and shout it three times
before you expect anyone to pay attention.

Yes I would, I'd like to sit and talk for a couple of hours
each day, I've not done much talking in the last few years.
I understand you're not from the Parole Board yes, and
nothing I say's going to affect my release date, either
bring it forward or put it back, because none of them will
hear it, right, understood. For a book. Often had the idea
you know I'd like to do a bit of writing myself. Suppose a
lot of people say that don't they? I remember from when I
was outside, you used to hear people say they'd always
like to write didn't they, if only they could find the time?
Funny isn't it: these places are full of folk who've got all
the time in the world. They're not doing anything and
they're not going anywhere, you'd think they'd all be
scribbling and writing away wouldn't you, producing a
million words a year? Suppose it's difficult though is it,
writing? People at school they're taught how to write in
the way of making marks on paper, and then they say 'I
can write' don't they? But all they mean's they can do
handwriting right? It'd be like learning sums and then
thinking you're a qualified accountant, that'd be the same
wouldn't it? In the way of writing like say an actual book

like, how do you start, how do you go about that?

No, right sure that's fine with me, yes sorry: talk about me first, and then at the end each day I ask you questions and things about writing, sure, sounds great.

Talk about myself. What does a thirty-year-old fat man who's been in prison since he was nineteen talk about though, that's the problem? Not much to say that's new is there? Prison yesterday, last week, last month, last year; prison tomorrow, next week, next month, next year. When was yesterday, what happened, I don't remember it? Due to general lack of interest tomorrow has been cancelled. Whatever point you're at, that's all you can say. Sometimes you get a wave of depression sweeps over you, other times you're just numb. Suppose it's the boredom more than anything, the monotony. There's no way of breaking it that I know of. That's not true strictly speaking now that I come to think of it, though. I used to, I don't do it now so much, but I used to kick off, that was my way of passing time. It's an expression means fighting, having punch-ups, causing trouble, getting yourself on punishment. I did it regularly till about last year sometime, matter of fact. You see the biggest punishment they can give you in prison, I mean the one that hurts you the most, is to take part of your remission away from you. Automatically on a fixed sentence you qualify for a third remission of it for good behaviour, so like if you're doing twelve months you're only actually going to do eight. If you behave badly, transgress, they make you do nine months instead, so taking four weeks' remission off of you, that's a lot. You'd been looking forward to being home for Christmas hadn't you, now you're not going home till the middle of January, that hurts.

That only applies if you're a fixed sentence man though, not if you're a lifer. You haven't got a fixed date for the end of your sentence, all you've got is a vague date when you might be released on licence. So there's nothing they can take away from you. They can only say to you 'Don't do that because it'll delay your date of parole.' Someone like me, when are we talking about? The year 2000? 'Don't do

that Robinson else we won't let you out until 2001'? It's a
joke isn't it? See what I mean?

So I did kicking off, punching the first person in the
throat that's passing, screw or con. I'd do it deliberately –
calculatingly, is that the word? Brought up in front of the
Governor, he says 'Robinson, you're going down on chokey
for a while.' I'd say 'Right sir, yes sir, thank you very much
sir, makes a change.' One of them, I think it was Long
Lartin, he said to me 'Robinson, I don't know what we're
going to do about you.' I said to him 'Well I do' I said
'you're going to put me on chokey you cunt.' He said 'Oh
yes I'm going to do that, I mean afterwards.' I said 'Put me
back on chokey again, right, what else is there?'

Rotten job, prison governor, don't know why they do it
most of them. I know why screws are screws, because
they're too thick to be anything else and no one'd give them
a decent job in anything. Governors though, some of them
are quite well-educated people. You can't think what pos-
sesses them can you, presiding over a shit heap like a
prison? Most of them you know, I really believe this, they
do genuinely think what they're doing is worthwhile, that it
contributes to the good of society. Which it might do,
insofar as it keeps thugs like me somewhere where they
can't do no more harm. But that could be done by trained
monkeys such as screws: you don't need a university degree
to keep people locked up. So where's the job satisfaction in
it for an intelligent man? I simply can't fathom it you know,
I really can't.

Hello, there's the dinner bell, I'd better go and get me
goulash before it's all gone. So when'll I see you then, two
o'clock tomorrow afternoon? Great, look forward to it. I'll
not be so nervous then.

– You want to hear about social standing? A bloke comes up
to me in the canteen today, he's a new arrival, and he comes
up to me and he says 'You Alan Robinson, somebody's just
pointed you out to me.' 'All right' I say, 'what if I am?' You

always have to be that bit cautious, see. He says, 'I was in the Scrubs, D Wing, when you was there, we never got to meet because you was off down on chokey all the time.' I said 'Yes, so, right, what?' He said 'You're the bloke killed a copper aren't you? Well put it there mate, congratulations, always good to meet someone who's taken one of the bastards out.' I said to him 'Have you ever killed a copper?' 'No' he said, 'I'm only doing six months for a bit of aggravated burglary.' 'So what are you congratulating me on then?' I said 'being in prison for twenty years?'

You can't understand the mentality of some people you know, can you? He's not thinking there's a mother somewhere who one day had a son she was proud of, a young lad joined the police force because he thought he might be doing some good in the world. I'm not going to get all sentimental about it because I'm not. I've never known much about him except his name and his age, but whoever he was and whatever he was, he didn't deserve what happened to him. Like the Judge said, it was a shocking waste of a life. Society's entitled to exact retribution, I don't think there could be any argument about that. But it was an accident, a hazard of his occupation, and of mine too in a way. When I say it was an accident I don't mean to say I didn't mean to kill him. It's true, of course I didn't: but I didn't mean not to kill him either, else I wouldn't have done what I done. I was determined to get away from him, I did get away from him, and it cost him his life. It cost me mine too as a result, and I think most people would say that's right, so it should, all square. But you try talking like that to that fucking lunatic who come up and shook my hand at dinner time. 'A bit of aggravated burglary'. Christ, what does he know about life? Probably held up a toy shop with a water pistol, something of that sort.

Yes that's right, you're right, I think it probably does have something to do with my size. People enjoy their fantasies about it. They probably think it was a desperate man encircled by a dozen uniformed police officers closing in on him, and he says 'Right well I'll take one of the bastards with me if I go.' So he picks up the nearest one and swings him over his head and then he chucks him off a scaffolding or something, and it takes all the other eleven in a pile on top of him before he's subdued.

Only it wasn't at all like that, not like that at all. I'd broken into a jeweller's shop in a shopping arcade in one of those new towns about midnight. Got in round the back and thought I was clever that I hadn't set the alarm off. Didn't know it was one of that new type though did I? Don't make a sound, work by infra-red and show up on the monitor in the security office. They press a button and a police patrol car's there in two minutes flat, you've not had any warning yourself at all. The first I heard's just a slight noise at the back, the same way I'd come in. I thought 'There's something here I don't like, I'm off out of this.' Step outside into the alley, and there's this young copper standing there with his torch. 'All right you' he says 'let's be having you, you're nicked.' I gave him a shove to get past him, then I started to leg it away as fast as I could. Apparently he radioed a short message for assistance and then set off after me. Fit young feller he was, I could hear him gaining on me. I ran out on to a path, it was dark but there was moonlight: I could see it was by a stream and there was a wood over the other side. I'd no idea how deep it was but I jumped in and the water only came to just somewhere about here over my ankles. He jumped in after me: right determined he was. When I got the other side I turned round, and we both stood there facing each other. I remember it very clearly: weird it was. The moonlight, this fair-haired lad quite a bit smaller than me, both of us standing there panting. He'd lost his helmet in the chase. I could feel there were stones under my feet and I bent down and picked one up. He wasn't scared; like I said, very determined, he just came on. I hit him on the head with the stone, and he went down on his face in the water.

I didn't stop to see how badly he was hurt, I was up the bank and away as hard as I could. Shit scared. They said in court he was a good swimmer and he'd drowned in two feet of water because he was unconscious in it face down. It was murder, you can't argue about that. I didn't know it at that stage though, only that I'd hit a copper with a brick, and hit him very hard.

Most of the night I was wandering around the outskirts of the town, hiding in doorways, it was raining. Next morning I went for a cup of tea, one of those caravan tea bars you see sometimes by the roadside. The woman in it had got a radio on somewhere up on a shelf, and there was the local news, all about this copper who'd been killed the night before. I knew what that meant: a copper killed anywhere, it means everyone in the world is going to be looking for you. I didn't finish my cup of tea, I left it cos I saw a long-distance coach coming along the road, so I ran out the layby and when it stopped I jumped on. Stupid things you do you see when you're scared out of your wits, don't you? That sort of behaviour, leaving your unfinished tea mug on the counter and running for a coach: the woman in the tea bar, she didn't need to be an idiot did she when someone did that? Right after it'd been on the radio they were looking for a man because a copper'd been killed.

I'd no idea where the coach was going, I hadn't looked. But it didn't stop for fifteen miles till it reached the bus station in the market place in the middle of a small town. Waiting there for it there were five police cars and half the county constabulary. And that was it. Not glamorous, not exciting, certainly not heroic, no way. As if I wasn't in enough trouble already. I was already on the run at the time from borstal too. 'Put it there mate, shake hands'. What a cunt.

— I didn't do anything last night. Usually I go down watch the telly on association, play a game of darts or something, read a magazine or a book. I just stayed in my cell and thought about what we'd been talking about. Not what you might call an inspiring story I told you was it? I get sick of myself sometimes, I really do. Where'd I finish, where'd we got to?

No I wouldn't say I was much of a villain beforehand, no. I mean I was a villain, but not one in the top division, nowhere like. Me and a few mates round my own age in the East End, we had this little firm, we did jobs together: shop breaking, warehouse breaking, stealing from vans, robbery. Nothing involving violence in fact, we was just your ordinary every-day thieves. I'm not saying we mightn't have been in time, but we were young, disorganized, more in it for a lark and a laugh than seriously in pursuit of riches. Dunno why par-ticularly in my case: a broken home, mum and dad divorced, mum off living with another man somewhere. But then it was the same for my older sister and brother wasn't it, and they were both straight. She grew up to be a typist with a firm of City solicitors, and he worked in a bank.

I was big for my age and popular. That might have something to do with being big: people like to be seen around with you, specially the girls. Not that I was violent, I wasn't. Matter of fact I didn't like violence, I kept out of it as much as I could, least till I got inside these places. People have the wrong idea you know, both inside prison and out. They think big equals tough. Up to a point it saves you trouble, people won't pick a fight with you. But if we're talking about sheer downright dangerous violence, my advice to anyone would be watch out for the little uns, they're the ones, people about your size. There's a bloke in here now, I've come across him a time or two before in the other nicks, name of Stan Norfolk: he's only four foot and a fag paper and nine stone wringing wet, but he's the most dangerous man I've ever known. Like everyone else when I see him coming I try and pretend I'm part of the furniture. What's so dangerous about him? Well let's put it like this, he's a walking stick of gelignite and you never know when he's going to go off: perhaps if he thinks you're laughing at him, or saying things behind his back, or just if you're making a draught. He doesn't have to have a good reason, or any reason at all come to that. Lays into you with his boots and his fists and his knees and his elbows and his head-butts, I tell you, he's terrifying. I hadn't been here long, he stopped me in the corridor one day, just stood there blocking the way with his hands on his hips. He said to me 'I suppose you think you're tough do you?' he said. 'Me?' I said, 'No I don't think I'm tough' I said. 'Matter of fact Stan I've taken up a new religion recently, it's called devout cowardice.' 'All right' he says, 'well you see you practise it and you'll be all right.' He's a one hundred per cent fully paid-up what do they call it, psychopath?

– It's funny you know, I have, I've thought really hard about it since you asked, and I can't think of anything much in the way of childhood memories at all. Funny isn't it? I remember the street where we lived in Canning Town, I remember my father working at the bus depot, I remember a bit about school but not much because I wasn't there half the time, and that's about the lot. I think I lived life off the top of my head, know what I mean? Roaming the streets with my mates, nicking sweets and stuff, joyriding in motors, but nothing else really at all. The old man as far as I can recollect it, he always used to be sleeping: not because he was lazy, but he did a lot of night-shift work, so the house had to be kept quiet for him during the day.

My sister stayed at home to look after him and me and my brother because him and our mother were divorced and she was living with her second husband; and I remember we was always being pushed out of the house so Dad could sleep. I think that's why there wasn't much schooling because she didn't care where we were so long as we weren't there, know what I mean? I think she was kind and I think she did her best, but it can't have been much of a life for her of her own. Where she got herself an education from and got a job in a solicitor's, that's something I'll never know. Made me start wondering if other people are the same, do you think they are? You know, never thinking back much about their childhood till someone asks them, then when someone does they don't know much at all and there's no one to ask and sort of fill it in.

My mother you know, I don't think I'd even recognize her now if she was to come walking in through that door. She must have left my father when I was dunno, five six or somewhere round there, and I only saw her once after that in the whole of the rest of my life. I say once but well one and a half times would be more like it strictly speaking.

I was sent to approved school when I was I think it was ten, I'm not sure of the exact age you could be put away in those days, but I know it was the youngest age you could qualify at. I'm not sure now what the offence or offences were either: truanting and nicking things I should think, like I was telling you about. I do remember I don't remember feeling a chip on my shoulder about it or anything of that sort, I think I thought going away was going to be a bit of good fun. You hear a lot about how they're breeding places for crime and so on, approved schools, but from what I can recall of it, this place wasn't like that. A big old house in the country somewhere it was, Essex or somewhere of that kind. They had chickens and goats and things, and cows, more or less like a little farm it was. The staff I remember they were all quite decent sorts of people, there was no bullying or anything of that kind. If you look at it from the point of view of whoever it was put me there, I've never thought anything but they were trying to do me a good turn. Mother gone off, father working nights, being brought up by a sister who herself can't have been more than about fourteen, running around the streets with a gang of lads thieving and the rest of it. You can see it was an effort to get me out of all that can't you, that's the way they looked at it.

Anyhow, one day at this approved school they told me I'd got a visitor come to see me, and they took me into a room and it was my mam. Course I didn't know her, I'd not seen her since I was little had I? She was all right and she talked to me, she said all the arrangements had been made when I come out of the approved school, I was going to go and live with her and this man she said was called my Uncle Geoffrey in their house at Clacton. I thought great, living at the seaside, I was well pleased wasn't I? She said I was to go home, and then in a few days after that they'd come and collect me from there.

Perhaps it was a week, could have been a fortnight later, anyway home I go and I'm dead excited about it. My dad said they'd talked about it and decided it was for the best, he was going to miss me but he'd come and see me, and my sister she said more or less the same. She said she'd help me get my things all packed up ready, Mam was coming on the Friday afternoon or whenever it was. You know what kids are like: my sister was washing and ironing clothes for me, but all I was worried about were the things like my football and one of those plastic aerodromes with all different models of planes. I think I had a Meccano or something of that sort too, all my West Ham posters and pop records and the rest of the gear. I wasn't worried about clothes, they came last on the list. There was such a pile of stuff I remember, my dad said we hadn't got a case anywhere near big enough, so he went out and bought a new one. Not an expensive one, he couldn't afford it, it was made out of painted cardboard I should think, know the sort I mean? It was enormous. My sister said that was it, we'd put in everything we could but anything after that would have to be left behind.

I remember I had it all packed up and ready for taking with me days before my mam was due to come, and everyone kept falling over it so we had to keep it out of the way under the kitchen table. I was forever pulling it out to put new things in, and throwing out things I'd decided I was going to leave behind. I remember it had those expanding metal hinges like, and the same on the locks on the front, do you remember them? I had it on the very last notch it would still fasten on, and my sister kept telling me if I tried to put any more in it it wouldn't stay shut, she got really narky with me about it.

At last the great day dawned as they say, and I was up I

don't know what time in the morning waiting for my mam. In the finish I think it was about two o'clock in the afternoon when she arrived. When my sister opened the door to her, she came in and she was very I don't know how to describe it, sort of cold and offhand with me. She said she wanted me to go in the front room and shut the door and wait, cos first she wanted to talk to my sister in the kitchen. I remember she didn't look at me directly, she said it to my sister. Tell him to stay in there and wait, things like that.

I went in the front room, and I could hear her and my sister talking in the kitchen, only it wasn't loud enough for me to hear what they were saying. I'm standing on one foot then the other, and then all of a sudden I hear the front door go. I'm out of the room like a streak and into the kitchen, and there's my sister just looks at me and gives a little sort of shrug to her shoulders like that, and she says 'She's gone.' You know what the thought was flashed through my mind? Funny the way kids' minds work isn't it? I did, I genuinely thought she'd forgotten me. So I dive under the table and I drag this whacking great suitcase out, and I charge off down the hallway and out of the front door doing my best to carry it, dragging it along. I look down the street and there's a motor with a man driving it, and my mam getting into it. So I go running as fast as I can with this great big case, and I'm shouting 'Heh Mam, wait for me, wait for me Mam, wait!' What I must've looked like, I can't imagine, really I can't. And this geezer in the car starts up his engine and he goes off like a bomb and they disappear round the corner. And it's just that moment of course isn't it the suitcase bursts open and everything in it spills out all over the pavement. Oh dearie me, you do you know haven't you, you've got to laugh?

— All that stuff the day before yesterday about prison culture, you must get tired of hearing about it. When you're a long-termer though, you don't know anything else. You live in it, it's all round you all day, it's all there is in your life, how can you be interested in anything else? Teach you the folly of a life of crime by shutting you away with a whole lot of others who have the same way of life? What do they expect? Cut you off from what contact you've ever had with the straight world outside and hope that's going to change you? Well I mean obviously it's not is it, how could it?

When I came inside I had what, a mother and father even if they were divorced, a brother and sister and a girlfriend, an uncle up in Derby and that was about it. What's that, one two three four five six, plus possibly two more. At first they all wrote and some of them came on visits: eight Christmas cards and birthday cards the first year, six the next, five or six the year after. Then my mam started getting fed up with it, or the man she lives with did; my father had a heart attack and's never recovered from it so he's not too agile, my sister got married and my brother got transferred to a job abroad. The girlfriend well obviously she'd meet up with another bloke, one day comes the Dear John. You can't blame the girl. I didn't like the part though where she said 'But I've asked another friend of mine to write to you instead of me, she's a nice girl and says she'll be happy to keep in touch with you.' Romance by proxy, by post. On top of all that they move you about from one prison to another: and it's a fact, they lose you. They do you know, fifty thousand men in prison and sometimes they lose track of you. Someone asks your address to write to you, and they can't tell them because they're not sure where you are. You yourself, you're bloody certain you don't know where you are. Pink walls in B Wing, this must be Lewes then, right? You ask a screw, he says No it's not mate, Lewes has gone environmental, it's all green now, this is Kingston Portsmouth. You say Well which, Kingston or Portsmouth, I'd read in the papers Greater London was spreading but I didn't know it's got as bad as that? Last year it had got down to two letters and one card, and I'd not had a visit from anyone since a year the June before.

Dinner bell again, see you two o'clock this afternoon, right. Wonder what it'll be for us today, roast pheasant and redcurrant jelly with asparagus and new potatoes, or sausage beans and chips?

— They fooled us good and proper today. It is Thursday isn't it, yeh that's what I thought. You know what they gave us? Cod and boiled potatoes. We all thought it must be Friday, it's Friday we have fish. Or perhaps there's no tomorrow, it's been cancelled owing to lack of interest. No, I don't know where I got that from, out of some book or other I suppose. So where did you go, what did you have for your lunch?

Interesting you see isn't it, you learn something new every day. A ham sandwich and a lager at the pub over the road eh? I didn't know there was a pub over the road, you've widened my geographical knowledge. A ham sandwich and a lager. Just for once now, if they came to me and said what would I like to do for a change, I'd say something like 'Let me go and have a ham sandwich and a lager somewhere. Give me an hour or an hour and a quarter, that's all, let me have an amble out on my own. I won't run away, I'll come back I promise, only let me have just an hour and a quarter somewhere else but this place.' Funny thing is you know, I would come back too, I really would. I'd be so scared now being outside on my own, I'd come back for my own safety I would.

Eleven years in prisons and a long lot more to come, that's a lot of imprisonment isn't it? How do you do it, how do you think you're going to get through it, what sort of person are you going to be at the end? Yes well right, as you say. Me who asked the questions so I'm the one should try and answer them. First of all I'd say you act tough, you let them see they're not going to break you, you'll keep your integrity of personality, you'll never bend the knee. That's what I did and I kept it up five years nearly six. It wasn't a waste of time though, you don't waste time in prison, you spend it.

Then one day a chap came down to talk to me, I think he

was an Assistant Governor, and I think it was in Preston or it might have been Parkhurst. He came in my cell down on chokey and he sat down and he said 'Well Robinson, go on then, tell me what you're doing.' You never like that approach you know, the reasonable sort, makes you dead suspicious. I told him to eff off out of it or I'd put one on him, or two if there was time before the screw outside came to his rescue. He said 'There isn't a screw outside, go and have a look.' I took him at his word and there wasn't. I said to him 'You're taking a risk mate aren't you, down here on your own with a known animal like me, what're you trying to do, win the Queen's Award for bravery in the face of a crime wave or something?'

Funny little bloke he was, bald head, middle-aged. I said 'Look mate, if you want a heart-to-heart, try talking to the wall.' He said no, he wasn't trying to get me to see the error of my ways or any of that. But did I want to go on being what I'd described myself as, a known animal he said: was that how I wanted to go on the rest of my life sentence? 'Because' he said, very quiet and calm like, he said: 'Because if you do, that's all right, we can contain you, make no mistake about that.' Then he got up and he slowly turned round and he walked out.

I stood there, you know, and you know what I did? I laughed. Not much, but I laughed. I thought 'That little bastard's just threatened me. And what've I done, have I picked him up and broken his back like I'd have tried to if he'd been a screw? No I haven't. Have I thrown my table against the wall and dragged my bed up against the door and barricaded like I'd normally have done? No I've not done that either, all I've done is stood here and seen the funny side of it and laughed.'

I'm not going to say it was a turning point or anything of that sort: it wasn't. I didn't say to myself from then on I was a reformed character. In fact I'd say if anything for a couple of months afterwards I was worse than I'd been before. Like I was kicking against thinking about what he'd been saying, know what I mean? But as it went on, those words of his though, they kept coming back into my head. 'A known animal': it was like I was saying 'Yes, yes, that's what I want to be, a known animal, yes!' I was trying to persuade myself wasn't I? Right; but now and again in the middle of rucking and smashing up and kicking off, just now and again I'd stop and I'd find I was having a little laugh at myself. Somehow or other after that I started to quieten down. Not a lot mind you, I mean I can still be a wild man if something takes me that way. Only not so much, not so often, know what I mean? On the outside I'm a hard man, or I put on a front that I'm one. Inside though, I'm not soft but I'm getting to be less like a kid.

I'll tell you something. Well I'll try and tell you something. I'll tell you something that . . . It's not easy, it's not an easy thing to say, specially not for somebody who thinks he's a bit of a tough guy. It sounds like weakness. Whatever way you look at it, however you say it, that's what it sounds like. Maybe because that's what it is. Weakness. I'll try and say it, but it's fucking difficult to say to you, it really is, I can tell you that.

It's that inside here, it hurts. Right down inside, down to deep inside of me, it hurts. When I go out of that door there and go down the corridor to the canteen for my tea, no one'll see it. All they'll see is the big fat bloke with the smile on his face, walking along swinging his arms. 'Hi Alan.' 'Hi Charlie.' 'All right Alan?' 'Sure mate, fine, how about you?' That'll be the outside: but inside here it's a hole, a big hollow empty hole, that's all, a big big hurt. I don't have any excuse for what I did and there's nothing I can do that will undo it . . . but oh Jesus mate how many times I've wished to God someone'd come along and tell me how I could. Society's taken its retribution on me like it's entitled to, but it's a whole lot harder than a lot of society's members think, if they ever do think about it. I took somebody's life away yes, and in return they're doing the same to me. Only their way of doing it is slowly day by day, relentlessly, bit by bit. Eating you away, shrinking you smaller and smaller, inch by inch, depriving you more and more of what's left of your personality and feelings, every shred of your individuality. If society would only say one day, one definite day, they'll take me back, that's all I want, for them to tell me that. Only for Christ's sake while there's still something left of me to take back.

I'm a big tough man to sit here and make an exhibition of myself like this crying aren't I yeh, a really big tough man?

– Well then, never got round to the subject of talking about writing did we in the end? A lot of things I'd liked to have asked you about it, still never mind. Letters you mean, put the questions in letters? Sure yeh why not, that'd be great. Don't get many letters these days or write them either, I'll enjoy that.

Six months later he enrolled in a correspondence course in Creative Writing, which he's still doing: and shortly afterwards put his name down for consideration for full-time education.

TWELVE

Marathon Man

FRANK JONES

At the end of the third-floor landing, through the barred window that stretched from ground to roof level of the prison wing, the modern red brick two-storeyed segregation block could be seen at the other side of the yard below. It was surrounded by a twenty-foot-high mesh fence topped with barbed wire, and had surveillance cameras on towers at each corner. The special unit: a prison within a prison.

In the weak March afternoon sunshine, a small dark-haired man, shirtless in too-large dungarees and grubby old tennis shoes, ran steadily round and round the block on the concrete path inside the perimeter fence. He kept his fists clenched, his elbows in and his arms working regularly like pistons, blowing out his cheeks as he regulated his breathing.

The big amiable Principal Officer stood watching from the landing for a while, then gave a nod of his head.

— There you are, he said. There he goes, that's him, that's our Frankie. Marathon Man. Come on, I'll take you across.

Slightly built and of medium height, he had crinkly brown hair and hazel-green eyes. A direct look, a friendly smile, a firm handshake, several missing front teeth and a broad rich York-shire accent. He was thirty-one.

— Aye I am, I'm still a bit puffed, don't fret though I'll be all reet. Will I sit 'ere? What's this then, an old cell or summat is it? Rum sort of room to set us in though, not room to swing a cat is there eh? Close though, shall us see if I can reach that window if I climb up ont table? Aye . . . I can just. Stuck, well that's typical. 'Alf a mo, that's got it. There that's better innit. Still don't let that much fresh air in though. Still.

Saw me running did you, oh aye? Done forty-nine times round the block this afternoon, I reckon I do that every day. Why forty-nine? Well once round's 180 yards see, so that's five mile more or less exact. Till now I do only afternoons, but next week I've got permission to do mornings and all. Then it'll be ten miles a day. I'm going to keep pushing it up a bit further each week, cos it's the Marathon next month. About the twenty-third is it, somewhere round there? The London Marathon. That's what we're in for: nineteen of us, sixteen cons and three members of staff.

We're doing it for charity, Children's Leukaemia Fund I believe it's called, some name like that. We've got outside sponsors and everything, reckon we'll raise a good few bob. Me, I'm aiming to complete the whole course, twenty-six miles and something yards is it? I don't see why I shouldn't, not with the practising programme I've worked out. Aye, it'll be same day it teks place in London starting same time and following exactly the same route. On a map I mean, one of the screws brought it in for us a few weeks back. I've got it all up here in me head though by now, I've been studying it. Ninety-eight circuits ten mile; 147 fifteen, 196 twenty, and another sixty-eight on top that'll see me home. Makes it more interesting, you think now I'm crossing Tower Bridge, now I'm in the Isle of Dogs, now I'm running down the Mall. Some says I'll not do it all, but I will. I'd have a bet I'll be the only one does and all. They say good stuff comes in little packages don't they eh?

They told me you'd like to come and talk with us, over a few days, is that right? Fancy. No I'm a bit surprised that's all, it's a good while since I've had a visitor. Folk's not exactly queuing up to meet me. Still. Well. Yes. All right.

– They said I could bring two of 'em in to show to you, so I've brought you the two what I think are me best. This windmill one, I got it from a photograph in a book. I think it's at a place in Norfolk somewhere, I believe they call it Thurne. I've never been. Anyhow I studied it very careful like, then I drew it out on paper what I thought the proportions might be. This side this long compared with the height, the back 'ere that long, then put it all on graph paper. Then when I started building it, it took me two month to mek it, then I put the paint on and varnished it like to give it a finish. I think it looks reet nice. The photograph I saw, it were black and white so I don't know what its real colour is. I've made it light brown, I should think it's that. The sails turn round you see, if you just do it like that with the tip of your finger. Then it swings round like this a bit and all, so's it can turn the direction the wind's coming from. One of the officers said let's try it int yard but I said no. It's too frail, one good strong puff of wind and it could be all smashed up. I taught myself how to do it; all told it took me two month to mek, there's 2,450 matchsticks in it.

Now this other one 'ere, this big ship, this one's got 5,600 matches in it, every one of 'em individually glued together. The windmill I cheated a bit, you know put four or five side by side and spread glue over; this one I thought no, fair do's, let's do it proper like it ought to be, each one separate one by one. I've not decided whether I'll paint it yet or not, I think it looks nice like it is, don't you? In me cell I've got a gypsy caravan, a lighthouse, a house with rooms in it, with a front lifts off so's you can see the little furniture inside, and a native canoe I've not finished yet. I think it's a nice hobby. All the officers, they all keep their burnt matches for me, they put 'em in a cardboard box in the office cupboard, and I can go and help meself whenever I like.

I'm glad you like them, I like them an all. I've got plans one day I might do Wakefield Trinity's Rugby League football ground. You know, all the terraces and seats, the roofs of the stand, everything right down to the last detail. That'd be a real big project that would, I'll say, not 'alf eh? Still, might get round to it one day.

Oh aye yes, rugby, that were all I ever wanted as a kid, leave school and play for Wakefield Trinity. I did get as far as having a trial with them, but nothing come of it. I were a prop forward. I weren't very tall but I were heavy: I were eleven stone where most of the lads my age, they were only about nine. And they said I had what they call a low centre of gravity. I were fast and all. Oh aye I would, I'd have liked to go professional but I just weren't quite that bit good enough. You've got to be reet good you know if you want to be professional at something.

No, I've no idea where I got it from, don't ask me, it weren't in the family or nothing like that. I think it were a master at school, he was a bit of a fanatic, I should think it was him most likely who got us keen on it. His name was Charlie Watson. I think he'd wanted to be a player himself in his day. I had a girlfriend and all, she used to come and watch me when I played for the school. Barbara Wallwork. You don't get many girls interested in sport so much. She didn't play anything herself but she liked to come an watch. Barbara Wallwork, eh? That's bringing things back a bit. Her mother and my mother, they were friends; one had a son and the other had a daughter, both round about the same age. Suppose they might have thought, you know, one day. Wonder what's become of her, married and got a nice house somewhere, a couple of kids I should think.

But I went to the bad I did. I started going to the bad right when I left school. I got in with a lot of lads my own age, a right mob we were, real badly behaved. I remember once we took a cricket bat into a Pakistani's grocery shop and threatened him with it while we helped oursells to his sweets and cans of beer and took all the money from out of his till. Frightened the life out of him, five or six rough lads late at night. Sounds right bad you know doesn't it, it is bad too, you shouldn't behave like that. I think we enjoyed the frightening part of it more than we needed the money too, the money were kids' stuff, only a few quid.

What we did do that got us money, a good lot of it, was we was in with a bloke had a boat shop over int next town. He supplied folk with yachts and gear and stuff like that, but most of all he sold them powerboat engines. He weren't the actual owner, just worked there. Whenever they sold a powerboat engine, that's several thousand quid's worth, he'd look in the book and see the name and address of the person who'd bought it: whether it'd been delivered to his boat or his house, then he'd pass it on to us. We'd go and have a recce, make sure it was there, then we'd nick a truck with lifting tackle from another boatyard, and go down at night and load up the engine. Then we'd tek it the other side of the Pennines, Manchester or Oldham or round there. There was another bloke there who was always in the market for that sort of gear. He'd give us a good price for it, and we'd split six ways with the feller who'd given us the tip. Only problem there though was the police get to know who specializes in doing what. They say to theirsells 'Missing powerboat engine? That'll be Roy Jackson and his lot.' Then they go round his house and they say to him 'Right Roy where was you last Tuesday night?' Course Roy's already got his alibi sorted out: his girlfriend swears he was with her all night, never put a foot out of bed. But one of the others in the mob, he's not been so clever. When the Law's on to him they say 'All right then Roddy, who else was with you? Tell us their names and each one you tell us we'll get you a year off your sentence.' That's how it goes. Still, you can't blame the bloke, not really.

I were one of the lucky ones. I could always prove where I was, I saw to that every time we went on a job. All I ever got before this was three years' probation. Mind you I wasn't regular at it, I think I was only in on a couple of jobs. I did my probation with no bother: I liked a bit of a drink now and again, but there were no real difficulty there. I weren't on probation for that, that weren't my problem, drink. Not to the probation.

— My problem when we stopped yesterday, yes well my problem you see were drink. An the even bigger problem still were nobody knew it, because I didn't let on. Not me mother, not me school teachers, the probation, not no one. Praps not even mesell, whether I let on to mesell, I don't know that. If I didn't get enough booze I weren't happy: if I did I were, and it were as simple as that. It sounds a thing to say that most folk couldn't believe, but I'd say I were an alcoholic from when I were twelve or somewhere around there.

There were a couple of other lads at school, Jimmy Entwhistle were one and the other I've forgotten his name. Jimmy Entwhistle, his mum she must have been an alcoholic too, because her house, well you can't imagine how much drink she had there. It seemed like you only had to open a cupboard and a bottle fell out. Under the stairs, in crates, the bedroom wardrobes, under the sink int kitchen, everywhere. I dunno what sort of a woman she were, whether she had a job for a living, a husband or what. I think meself she were probably on the game, but for a schoolkid you never have too much idea really about grown-ups and mostly you don't ask.

I know we used to go round Jimmy Entwhistle's most days after school and help ourselves to the drink. Empty bottles you see, that were another thing I remember, empty bottles standing around everywhere. If you finished one you just stood it among the others and it never got noticed. The stuff I liked the best, the only stuff I drank at all ever really, were sherry. That was something she were never short of were cheap sherry. I could drink, well I reckon I could drink nearly a bottle of that a day. And thing about it were it never had no after-effect: I'd get rolling drunk with it, then I'd just curl up somewhere and sleep it off, and then when I woke up I'd be right as rain. No headache, no tummy ache, nothing, not the slightest thing. Another good thing to it too were in between times, if I had to do something like go out with the lads on one of those boat engine stealing jobs, or nicking something else, I wouldn't drink at all, I'd stay stone sober. When it were necessary to have a clear head I had a clear head, then after it were over I'd drink myself stupid.

Same as with rugby, if I were playing a match I'd not touch a drop till the game were over. I've read about some others in the paper sometimes, these big professional sportsmen, footballers and cricketers and that. You read about how they get brought to court for drink driving and things, and banned from driving. Folk say 'Well how could he drink that much and stay fit to play his football or cricket?' I can understand that, I can: I were exactly the same. The only one bad effect it did have though, were it made me violent. When I were drunk I were violent, only I didn't remember it. Folk'd tell me of things I'd done, and I'd have no recollection of it at all. I could be in a fight say, and then remember nothing of it. I seemed to go wild.

It were a good life you know, drinking all that drink, playing sports and a bit of thieving. I remember Peggy saying to me once, she said to me one day 'Frank' she said, 'Frank you're always behaving like you hadn't a care in the world.' 'I haven't' I said to her, 'that's true, I haven't a care in the world.' As a kid, as a schoolboy, right up to when this happened, I was always happy-go-lucky, that'd be the word I'd use about myself. I remember never being sad about anything. Perhaps I should have been, praps that was what brought me in here. If I'd been sadder I might not have ended up where I am. Still you can never tell though can you?

I remember once two years ago when me mother came to see me, just before she were taken bad. We were talking, it were in the visiting room and it'd been a real nice visit up till then; and then all of a sudden she burst out crying. I said 'What's the matter, are you all right? What're you crying for, everyone's looking at you?' She said 'I'm sorry, I can't help it Frank, now and then it catches up with me, I feel so bad I didn't do right by you.' 'Not do right by me?' I said. 'What're you talking about? I had a very happy childhood I did, no one could say different.'

When I were thinking about it after, I think she had a bit of an unhappy life herself though. Me dad got killed in the coal mines, she had to go to work to bring me up, then I started getting into trouble, then I went wandering off and she didn't hear nothing from me for two year or more and didn't know where I were. Then all this business and now she hasn't got me, then this what do they call it multiple sclerosis and she can't come and see me no more. It's a lot for one person isn't it all that? I think her happiest time was probably Peggy and the kids, she always used to like it if they come for tea on a Sunday.

Who, Peggy d'you mean, how did I meet her? Oh, just like you do you know, one day at a bus stop. It were raining and there were this sort of glass shelter place and I were sitting in it and she come in to wait for the bus. I'd had a good bit to drink that day and I were sort of sitting there with me head back dozing. She started making fun of me, she says 'Well a right state you're in aren't you, you've drunk far too much haven't you, how d'you know it'll be the right bus when it comes?' I said I didn't mind, I weren't really waiting for a bus, I didn't mind if one came or not. Just then one was coming so 'Come on' she says, 'you'd better come along with me, we'll get a cup of coffee or summat, try and sober you up.' So she grabs me by the arm and pulls me on the bus with her.

She were a nice girl were Peggy: she'd be nineteen then, same age as me. I think she thought she could turn me into something, get me into good ways. They do don't they women sometimes. She were a hairdresser and I used to go with her to these modelling things they have, hairdressers have a competition to see who's the one who'd done the best new style. She went in for quite a few of them: Blackpool, Morecambe, Scarborough, Rotherham, all over the shop. She won some of them too. She used to make me put a suit on and promise her not to drink till after, and I always kept it. She called me her lucky mascot. She earnt good money, we stayed in a good class hotel: the people she worked for would pay all her expenses and she'd pay for mine, so I were happy.

Then we found Sarah were coming along, so we had to start thinking what'd be the best for us to do. I said we'd get married and I'd get a job. The first part of that were all right but not the second. We went and lived at her ma's and I got

odd jobs in the painting and decorating. But I weren't very
reliable about going home on pay day with me wage packet,
I'd sooner be down the pub with the lads. Her mother used
to get mad about it and mine did too, but not Peggy, she
didn't, she were always very understanding about it. I did
knock her about a bit, like I said I were violent. But then
after I didn't remember it. She said I'd got a problem, she
wanted me to see somebody and get help for it. She used to
tell her ma it was no use shouting at me, she should try and
help.

I did have a few jobs in between times, I can say that for
meself. But it seemed like as soon as I got a bit of money
in me hand I couldn't resist going in the pub. Peggy used
to come and get me out sometimes before all the
housekeeping were gone. When Sarah were born we sat
down and had a talk, and Peggy said well in a few months
she'd go back to her hairdressing job, her mum'd look
after the baby, and I could go on trying to straighten meself out. We decided though in the meantime like since
there didn't seem all that amount of work around where
we was living, it'd be better if I went away for a while and
got jobs as I was moving about. Casual labouring on building sites, tarmacking the roads, things like that. I'd not
been too happy with her ma, her and me'd never really got
on like, so it were best I went.

They don't half make a racket don't they them seagulls
we can hear squawking all the time? Is this prison somewhere near the sea then is it? No I've no idea where it is.
Not near the sea at all? Rum do that is then isn't it then,
seagulls?

Well, Peggy and me, will I go on for a bit? That idea of
me going off looking for work, I think another idea she
might have had in mind were it might tek me away from me
drinking pals. It didn't though, wherever you go you can
always get yourself drinking pals can't you, specially if
you've got a few bob in your pocket? First off, I did get
some labouring jobs, and some hotel work, kitchen porter
and things. I did go home with a bit of money in me pocket

now and again, say once a fortnight about. When it come Sarah was about three or four month, Peggy went back to her hairdressing so she'd no worries about money coming in no more. Every time I went back she was always nice and friendly, but I think she'd given up on me really. Sometimes I think back to it and do you know what I think? I think I were having one of them what they call nervous breakdowns, very long drawn out. Drinking, wandering around, sleeping rough all the time, not knowing where I were. I think it must've been something of that sort, would you say so too? Yeh, I mean a nice home to go to, a nice wife who'd be happy for me not to try to go out to work even, a nice kiddy. Yet whenever I went back, I couldn't stand it more than a few days, a week at the outside, then I'd be off.

It went on that way over a year. When Peggy told me she were having another baby, I could see it all coming back again where I'd have to live at home and try and support her again. So I were off again and that time I didn't go back home for close on two year. Well I say I didn't go back for two year, what I mean is I didn't go back no more at all. It were two year and then I got arrested for this.

I'm just trying to see your watch, does it say four o'clock? I'd best be going then, the PO said if I wanted to see the video I were to be outside his office by four o'clock. It's one he's brought in for me and a couple of the other Rule 43s, the rugby match last Saturday he recorded.

See you tomorrow then. It gets bad tomorrow, tomorrow it gets very bad indeed. Still, it's got to be all or nothing hasn't it?

Rule 43 allows the prison authorities to keep a prisoner in solitary confinement 'for reasons of good order and discipline'. It's used sometimes to give a recalcitrant and violent man the opportunity to have what's described as 'a cooling-off period'. Prisoners themselves claim not to be able to differentiate between this and punishment; especially when it's accompanied by loss of earnings, loss of remission, and loss of privileges such as association with other prisoners.

'Good order and discipline' however may not cover only the behaviour of the prisoner himself. It can be and more often is construed to apply to the possible behaviour of other prisoners towards him if he's mixing freely with them: he could well be a target for physical attacks of a violent and vicious kind. A man on Rule 43, in perpetual solitary confinement, is usually there for his own protection. Frank Jones has been on Rule 43 since the day of his arrest.

He has so far served four years of two life sentences for the murder of an eight-year-old boy and, three months later, of a three-year-old girl. Neither was known to him: he came across the boy playing on his own in a wood, and he abducted the girl late at night from her bedroom in a mobile home on a run-down site while her parents were in a nearby caravan with neighbours. Both the killings were accompanied by battering, strangling and severe sexual assault. One child's body was found in a ditch, the other on a rubbish tip. In passing sentence the Judge made a recommendation that the possibility of his release from custody should not be even considered for at least twenty-five years.

– The traffic lights is the thing I remember clearest, traffic lights along the road, a long way away up at the top of the hill. I couldn't see properly what they were, I couldn't make them out. It were pitch dark, two or three o'clock in the morning, no street lamps or nothing, it were in the country. I could see this red light like in the distance, it kept disappearing then another light came in its place as I were walking towards it. Red, then yellow, then they disappeared and there were a green one. I couldn't make out what were going on. Suspended lights in the air they were, high up because they were on a hill.

The other thing I remember's the stink and all this oil all over me on me hands and face and in me hair. The more I tried to wipe it off the more everywhere it went on me clothes. Walking in the dark towards the traffic lights, getting nearer and nearer to them till they were bright enough to see by, and I could see this stinking stuff all over me looking first red, then yellow then green. It was like I'd been knocked down in a motor accident, I thought that at first. Your mind's a blank, like you've been knocked unconscious or something. Then you suddenly come to and it starts to come back: and you know you've done something terrible, terrible. And you think Oh Christ, what've I done?

I went in a field somewhere, then I curled up and went to sleep. Next morning it was very cold, misty like it can be in the summer before it starts being a hot day. I walked a mile or two, then there was a park: it had public toilets by the gate, so I went in to see if I could get a wash. There was only cold water but I got most of the oil off me. What I must've done the night before was washed meself in a tank of water standing somewhere, only it was dark and I couldn't see it were some sort of waste tank with all oil in it.

When I'd cleaned myself up a bit in the toilets I walked along the road some more past a golf course. Then a lorry come along, a milk tanker I think it were, and the driver gave me a lift. He said 'You look rough mate, what's happened to you?' I said I'd been in a fight and asked him to drop me off before we got to the next town. I waited for a lift in another direction, it took me near all the way to Birmingham I think. The next night again sleeping in a field; I was hungry but I didn't dare go in nowhere so I stayed out all night. I was desperate for a drink but I couldn't risk going nowhere for a drink either.

It were around lunch-time the next day, somewhere there, the police car stopped as I were walking along this country road. They picked me up and took me in, and said I were to wait for another lot of police coming for me from down south. They give me something to eat and I slept. They weren't bad to me. Then the other lot came and they took me to Luton down south. When we got there they started questioning me, different ones asking me questions, tekkin it in turns. They said 'Tell us about it Frankie, we know it was you Frankie, come on now Frankie tell us about it or we're going to beat the shit out of you.' I said 'No.' I said 'No I don't know nothing about it, not me no, it was nothing to do with me.' They just go on and on: all night, all the next day. I said 'It wasn't me, no, I don't know nothing about a little girl at all.' They said 'How'd you know it were a little girl we're asking you about Frankie, how'd you know that, how'd you know we're not asking you about a little boy?' 'No. It weren't me. No. It must've been someone else, it weren't me, no, no.'

How can you confess to something like that? You don't remember. Your mind won't let you: it can't. Never.

– I were all told eleven month on remand waiting for trial. They put me on Rule 43, solitary confinement for your own protection, but I still had a rough time like you do. There's all sorts in a big remand prison, bank robbers, terrorists, people in for big violence, they'll all think up ways of getting to you if they can. The screws are rough tongued with you, tell you you're a nonce, a sex maniac, a piece of shit doesn't deserve to live and stuff like that. But I've never had physical violence given to me by a screw. They don't need to, they just leave your cell door open when it's supposed to be locked, or look the other way on the landing when two or three are on to you. I had some bad beatings on remand. Six times, seven. Not so many since though, only a couple. That's where some of these teeth went.

I only had one visit while I was waiting trial, that was me mum. She came to see me but she just sat there looking at me, it was like she couldn't speak. They'd told her there was going to be another charge, the boy from three months before. I didn't remember that one, not nothing about it at all. It might not have been me. They said I was there in that town on that date, they could prove it, so it must have been. So in the finish I said oh all right then what was the difference, I was going down for the little girl anyhow. I still don't think it were me though, not the little boy.

After I were sentenced I wrote me mam three times, but she just blanked me. Then she wrote me a note, all it said were 'Please Frank don't write no more.' There were another letter in with it too to the Governor, he read it me. It were from Peggy: by then we was divorced. It said to him would he tell me all the arrangements had been made, she'd got married again and the bloke and her were leaving the next week, they were taking the kids to start up a new life with them in South Africa. She wasn't leaving no forwarding address. That's how it goes, you can understand it though can't you? Still.

The last year or so me mam, she has come round a bit, she did come once and see me. She said there weren't much she could do for me, she'd come and see me though when she got a bit better and felt up to it more. She's not got better though, she's got worse the welfare said, so I don't reckon I'll see her again no more.

What should happen to me now? Well I've got no idea. Prison's to learn you a lesson, isn't it? They can't ever let me out can they, because I do things you see. Do they keep people in prison for ever? I don't think much about that side of it, really, there's no point to it. I've done four year coming up to five, and that Judge he said at least twenty-five year. At least: that means before they were even to start considering me. So let's see, I'm thirty-one now so that means I'd be well gone sixty by then doesn't it?

I'm best behind me door making them matchstick models. But I'd like to keep up with the running and all if I could. It's good that is, I enjoy it. I'll see what time I do this year, then next year try and up it a bit, make it a sort of target like. They call me that here you know, the officers do: they call me 'Marathon Man'.

The amiable big Principal Officer reached down under his desk and brought up a smart plastic carrier bag with a local department store's prestigious name on it. He lifted out a pair of tissue-paper-wrapped sturdy green wellington boots from it and stood them on the blotter in front of him.

   – Wife's Christmas present for next Christmas, he said. I know it's only March still, but when I saw them in the shoe department at lunch-time I thought, Well come November or December they'll all be gone. I know she's always wanted some. Derri boots they call them, I wonder why they call them that?

   He looked at them, tilting his head a little from one side to the other, pleased.

   – Strange chap our Frankie isn't he, he said. What did you make of him?

Acknowledgements

It would not have been possible to do this book without the help of a great many people.

I was fortunate enough to be awarded a Simon Research Fellowship at the University of Manchester to do the preparatory work involved, and for the year I was there I was supported and encouraged by Professor Paul Wilding of the Department of Social Policy and Social Work, and by Dr Ken Pease, Reader in Criminology. I'm more than grateful to both of them. I also acknowledge generous help in the form of a Research Fellowship grant from the Leverhulme Trust, which provided me with later financial assistance enabling me to complete the writing.

I was given extensive assistance and co-operation by numerous probation services and their officers – particularly those of Inner London, Greater Manchester, Merseyside, Nottinghamshire, North Wales, Kent, Suffolk, Norfolk, Essex, Middlesex, West Midlands, Surrey, Avon, Hereford and Worcester, Rochdale and South West London. I thank all of them, as I do prison staff at Askham Grange, Gloucester, Bristol, Wakefield, Long Lartin and Frankland, County Durham. I also received help from the National Association of Probation Officers, the National Association for the Care and Resettlement of Offenders and the Prison Reform Trust.

Laurie Scudder, Head of the Life Sentence Section (P2) of the Home Office Prison Department, and his assistant Pam Curtis, were both endlessly helpful. So too were many other individuals in many different ways, including Professor Terence Morris, Louis Blom-Cooper QC, Assistant Chief Probation Officer Steve Murphy, Harry Crewe, Linda Saunders and Malcolm and Jackie Peet. Linda Ginn typed and retyped the final manuscript swiftly and immaculately, and Carol Moy again photocopied and collated it perfectly. At Seckers, Vicki Harris was the perfect editor, the best I've ever had. My agent Gill Coleridge supported me as always, and my wife Margery also did considerable research for me as well as giving her love and care.

So, to everyone mentioned here, my affectionate thanks. But my deepest debt of gratitude of all, of course, is to the people who agreed to be interviewed. It is impossible to estimate what it must have cost them to speak as they did, so bravely and frankly about themselves, their situations, their lives, and the deaths of others that they caused. I have changed their names and altered geographical locations, but nothing else. I hope they will feel I have represented fairly what they said: to each of them I give grateful thanks and much respect.

Tony Parker
Manchester/Suffolk
1987–1989

10 Rillington Place

The incredible but true story of how British justice
hanged an innocent man

Ludovic Kennedy

In 1950 Timothy Evans was hanged for murder. Sixteen years later
he was granted a free pardon. This is the book that cleared his
name.

'A very remarkable book. The first complete account in narrative
form of the lives of Evans and Christie and the tragic and pitiful end
to which they both came. Questions of grave public importance are
involved, but it is the brilliant way in which this complicated and
controversial story is told that makes it one of the most engrossing
and fascinating books of its kind. As a work of fiction it would have
been hailed as a great crime story; as a transcript from real life it
holds the reader under a kind of spell . . . as an example of human
nature under a microscope, this book, once taken up, cannot easily
be put down'   Lord Birkett, *Observer*

ISBN 0 586 03428 5

'Let Him Have It, Chris'
The Murder of Derek Bentley

M. J. Trow

With an introduction by Ludovic Kennedy

On 11 December 1952, Christopher Craig and Derek Bentley were found guilty of the murder of a policeman, Sidney Miles. Although it was Craig who shot Miles, it was Bentley who was condemned to hang. This man had an IQ of 66 and a mental age of nine . . .

The case against Craig was cut and cried. He killed and showed no remorse. But Bentley offered no resistance to the police on capture. What took him to the gallows, by making him an accomplice, was his shout to Craig: 'Let him have it, Chris', witnessed by three policemen. This disturbing book offers startling evidence that Bentley never uttered those words at all.

Never has a trial aroused such divided public feeling, Bentley's plight becoming one of the twentieth century's *causes célèbres*. This book, at last, puts the record straight.

'Nobody reading this book can seriously doubt Trow's conclusion that Bentley was wrongly convicted'   *Sunday Times*

ISBN 0 586 21262 0

Blood on the Thistle
A Casebook of 20th Century Scottish Murder

Douglas Skelton

From the Borders to the Highlands, Scotland has had more than its fair share of macabre murders . . .

The man who dismembered his wife and dumped the pieces across Central Scotland . . . the axeman who went berserk in a mental hospital . . . the shadowy killer who stalked Glasgow's dance halls . . . an infernal love triangle that led to murder . . . the 'demon butler' whose polite manners hid a lethal secret . . .

These are just a few of the stories in this book about the men and women who have sprinkled blood on the thistle of Scotland, killing through greed, fear, anger, lust or sheer hatred. Their stories are chilling, blood-curdling and terrifying – and they are all true.

In this compelling crime collection, Glasgow journalist Douglas Skelton has gathered together twenty such sinister tales of Scottish murder and its detection, from the infamous Peter Manuel and the cop-killing Howard Wilson to Brian Newcombe, the smooth-talking Casanova conman and the still unsolved mystery of 'Bible John'.

ISBN 0 00 638360 2

A Blood Betrayal

The Inside Story of the Jersey Murders

Barry Wood

For Nick and Elizabeth Newall, the middle-class dream of a carefree life in the sun had come true. Wealthy, happy and devoted, they were apparently doted on by their good-looking intelligent sons Roderick, an army officer, and Mark, a young City banker.

But underneath the façade was a terrible reality, for the Newalls were being rent apart by greed and mindless hatred. When their parents disappeared after a family dinner in 1987 their glamorous sons inherited the family millions.

Now, with their parents' bodies discovered in a shallow grave, Roderick Newall's flight from justice has come to a dramatic end.

With exclusive access to all the chief protagonists, including Newall himself, Barry Wood reveals

- why the murders went unsolved for 5 years
- how Roderick's single-handed voyage round the world culminated in arrest on the high seas
- how he nearly walked free after a dirty courtroom battle in Gibraltar

Authoritative, revealing and utterly compelling, this is classic true crime reading at its best.

ISBN 0 00 638375 0

The Profession of Violence

The Rise and Fall of the Kray Twins

New Edition

John Pearson

Reggie and Ronald Kray ruled London's gangland during the 1960s with a ruthlessness and viciousness that shocks even now. Building an empire of organized crime such as nobody has done before or since, the brothers swindled, intimidated, terrorized, extorted and brutally murdered. John Pearson explores the strange relationship that bound the twins together, and charts their gruesome career to their downfall and imprisonment for life in 1969.

Now expanded to include further extraordinary revelations, including the truth about the unusual alliance between the Kray twins and Lord Boothby – the Tory peer who won £40,000 damages in a libel settlement when he denied allegations of his association with the Krays – *Profession of Violence* is a truly classic work.

'The most famous biography of criminal life to have been published in Britain . . . it has become something of a cult among the young'   *Time Out*

'All credit to Mr Pearson for a brave and disturbing book'
                                                                                 Daily Express

ISBN 0 00 638371 8